THE ENDLESS MIRROR

Think,
Dream,
Draw,
Write,
Click, Click, Click!
♡ Mom
1999

THE ENDLESS MIRROR

REFLECTIONS ON OUR YESTERMORROW

Jack Folsom & Friends

Thomas Y. Crowell Company
NEW YORK   ESTABLISHED 1834

Copyright © 1974 by John B. Folsom

Designed by Jack Folsom & friends, Ingrid Beckman and
Judith Barry

Manufactured in the United States of America

1   2   3   4   5   6   7   8   9   10

Library of Congress Cataloging in Publication Data

Folsom, Jack.
    The endless mirror.

    1. Quotations, English. I. Title.
PN6081.F54   808.88'2   73-20343
ISBN 0-690-00280-7 (hardbound)
ISBN 0-690-00526-1 (paperbound)

COPYRIGHT
ACKNOWLEDGMENTS

The publisher wishes to thank the following for permission to use excerpts from copyrighted material and photographs of works of art (page numbers refer to THE ENDLESS MIRROR):

Allyn and Bacon, Inc.: excerpt on p. 136 from *Creative Teaching of the Language Arts in the Elementary School* by James A. Smith, copyright © 1967 by Allyn and Bacon, Inc., Boston, Mass.

Amherst College Collection: see credit on p. 72.

Art Institute of Chicago: see credit on p. 58.

Atheneum Publishers: "Economy" (p. 91), from *The Moving Target* by W. S. Merwin, copyright © 1963 by W. S. Merwin; "A Glimpse of the Ice" (p. 57) from *The Lice* by W. S. Merwin (appeared originally in *The Atlantic Monthly*); excerpt on p. 142 from *The Margaret Rudkin Pepperidge Farm Cookbook* by Margaret Rudkin, copyright © 1963 by Margaret Rudkin.

Bantam Books, Inc.: excerpts on pp. 3, 49, 167, 170–171 from *The Medium Is the Massage* by Marshall McLuhan and Quentin Fiore.

Benjamin Blom, Inc.: reproductions on pp. 35, 62, 68, 106, 132–133, 157, 179, 196, 204 from *The Works of James Gillray*, Benjamin Blom edition, 1968.

Brandt & Brandt: "Nightmare Number Three" (pp. 164–165) by Stephen Vincent Benet, from *The Selected Works of Stephen Vincent Benet*, Holt, Rinehart and Winston, Inc., copyright 1937 by Stephen Vincent Benet, copyright renewed © 1964 by Thomas C. Benet, Stephanie B. Mahin, and Rachel Benet Lewis.

George Chambers: "Deleightful Pie" (pp. 54–55) by George Chambers, reprinted in *The Iowa Review*, *The Wisconsin Review*, and in *Beowulf to Beatles* (New York: Free Press division of The Macmillan Co.).

Columbia University Libraries: "The System Investigates Itself" (p. 71) by Boardman Robinson, from *The Liberator*, March 19, 1921.

The Detroit Institute of Arts: see credit on p. 80.

Doubleday & Co., Inc.: excerpt on p. 43 from *The Floating Opera* by John Barth, copyright © 1967 by Doubleday & Co., Inc.; "I Knew A Woman" (p. 214) from *Collected Poems of Theodore Roethke*, copyright © 1954 by Theodore Roethke.

The Escher Foundation, Haags Gemeentmuseum, The Hague: reproductions on pp. 37, 91, 175, 207, 228, 231 from *The Graphic Work of M. C. Escher*.

The Galerie St. Etienne, New York: see credit on p. 160.

Hart Publishing Co.: excerpts on pp. 25, 62 from *Summerhill: A Radical Approach to Child Rearing* by A. S. Neill, copyright © 1969 Hart Publishing Co., New York.

Hafner Publishing Co., Inc., New York: excerpt on p. 63 from *The Principles of Morals and Legislation* by Jeremy Bentham.

Harcourt Brace Jovanovich, Inc.: excerpts on pp. 94, 103 from *The Zen Koan* by Isshū Miura and Ruth Fuller Sasaki, copyright © 1965 by Harvest Books, Harcourt Brace Jovanovich, Inc.; excerpts on pp. 217, 218 from *The Diary of Anaïs Nin*, Vol. II.

Harper & Row, Publishers, Inc.: excerpt on p. 44 from *People in Quandaries* by Wendell Johnson, copyright © 1946 by Harper & Row, Publishers, Inc.

The Hispanic Society of America: see credit on p. 129.

Holt, Rinehart, and Winston, Inc.: excerpts on pp. 144, 161 from *Steppenwolf* by Hermann Hesse, copyright 1929, copyright © 1957 by Holt, Rinehart, and Winston, Inc.

Alfred A. Knopf, Inc., and Random House, Inc.: quote by Michel Carrouges (p. 213) from *The Second Sex* by Simone de Beauvoir, copyright © 1952, 1957 by Alfred A. Knopf, Inc.; excerpts on pp. 23, 66, 155, 223 from *Love's Body* by Norman O. Brown, copyright © 1966 by Alfred A. Knopf, Inc., and Random House, Inc.; excerpts on pp. 185, 186 from *The Fall* by Albert Camus, trans. Justin O'Brien, copyright © 1957 by Alfred A. Knopf, Inc., and Random House, Inc.; excerpt on pp. 174–175 from *Ulysses* by James Joyce, copyright © 1934 by Alfred A. Knopf, Inc., and Random House, Inc.; excerpt on p. 60 from "Sunday Morning," from *The Collected Poems of Wallace Stevens*, copyright © 1954 by Alfred A. Knopf, Inc., and Random House, Inc.

Little, Brown and Co.: excerpts on pp. 135, 187 from *The Aristos* by John Fowles, rev. ed., 1970.

Liveright Publishers, New York: excerpts on pp. 69, 166 from *The*

Ishmael Reed: "Beware: Do Not Read This Poem" (p. 178) by Ishmael Reed, from *Soulscript*, ed. June Jordan, copyright © 1970 by Doubleday & Co., Inc.

Shambala Publications, Berkeley and London: mandala on p. 177 from *Mandala* by José and Miriam Arguelles, 1972.

The Sierra Club: excerpts on pp. 112, 119, 120 from *This Is the American Earth* by Nancy Newhall and Ansel Adams, copyright © 1960 by The Sierra Club.

Simon & Schuster, Inc.: excerpts on pp. 160, 189 from *Report to Greco* and *St. Francis* by Nikos Kazantzakis, copyright © 1965 and copyright © 1962, respectively, by Simon & Schuster, Inc.

Gary Snyder: "Grace for Love" (p. 36), reprinted by permission of the author.

Gunther Stuhlman (author's representative): excerpts on pp. 67, 150, 183 from *House of Incest* by Anaïs Nin, published by The Swallow Press, Chicago, copyright © 1936, 1958, by Anaïs Nin.

The Viking Press, Inc.: "Shadows" (pp. 6–7), from *The Collected Poems of D. H. Lawrence*, ed. Vivian de Sola Pinto and F. Warren Roberts, copyright © 1964, 1971 by Angelo Ravagli and C. M. Weekley, Executors of the Estate of Frieda Lawrence Ravagli; excerpts on pp. 88, 138, 140, 197 from *Death of A Salesman* by Arthur Miller, copyright © 1949 by Arthur Miller, all rights reserved.

Dana Ware: poem on p. 234, reprinted by permission of the author.

Warner Brothers Music: see credit on p. 70.

Wellesley College Art Museum, Jewett Arts Center, Wellesley, Mass.: reproduction on p. 5.

The publisher would also like to acknowledge the following sources:

School of Michelangelo, "Head of A Woman" (p. 61), British Museum, London.

Jörg Muscat, "Emperor Maximilian I" (p. 84), Kunsthistorisches Museum, Vienna.

Illustration from a mid-thirteenth-century psalter (p. 94), Duke of Rutland Collection, Belvoir Castle.

Four lines by Ryôkan (p. 209) from *Zen in English Literature and Oriental Classics* by R. H. Blyth.

PREFACE

In keeping with the theme and main approach of THE ENDLESS MIRROR, we should present more than one voice, even in the preface. What I have to say will be periodically offset by interjected remarks by c.l. white, whose perspectives and emphases differ somewhat from my own.

Let us begin with the idea of the mirror.

J.F.: In the Middle Ages and Renaissance, a Mirror was a life story or collection of life stories, told to show how the Wheel of Fortune turns, how the Mighty fall in their turn, and how the reader, by seeing his own reflection in the story, can take a lesson from it. Most devastating of all in the Mirror tradition was the part where the skull, stripped of life and flesh, was held up to view as a grim reminder of the ultimate Fate of all. *Mirres vous y*—"Behold yourself therein!" Behind the Now-life of every man and woman lies an endless succession of ancestors, earlier versions of oneself, stretching back to our common ancestors. From them have come to us the myths and archetypes that control our unconscious as well as conscious lives. Our recognition of ourselves in them is sometimes dim, sometimes sharp. We are not isolated from our common humanity, in spite of our differences and our contentions.

So we recognize ourselves in the endless mirror—so what? Small comfort if it is a reflection of despair, destruction, death, or even worse—absurdity. Better to be rid of the mirror and to swim away in some illusion-wave of change, of separation from the past. The wave carries us to a new world (perhaps?) of stately pleasure domes, of instantaneous telecommunications, of grief therapy in the mortuary of our beloved. But can we so arrogantly break the mirror of our past selves? Especially when it holds not only the image of Death, but also the image of Life? Some people struggle to affirm something permanent in the midst of flux and change, something more rewarding to contemplate than just *cogito, ergo sum.* But the affirmation cannot be seen without the denial: You cannot deny death, but in order to affirm life, you must deny destructive acts. You cannot deny that destructive acts do occur, but you can deny that they *should.* Likewise, you can affirm once more what no one denies, but which is often forgot: We are spiritually as well as biologically a part of Nature, frail and vulnerable to be sure, a tissue of oppositions and contradictions, but in each life we are given a choice of *Eros* (love, unite, create), or *Thanatos* (reduce, destroy, die). Which instinctive force will dominate? Without another Mirror-book to prod us, our natural urge to release grip and perish would seem to win out. Why else do we club and rape our people? Why else do we hide behind locked doors?

> *c.l.w.:* The hope we present in this book is founded on the metaphysical principle that life is cyclical, that regardless of how man and his mind came into being, he is capable of generation and regeneration, creation and re-creation. But to create, man, who is the artist, the poet, the dreamer, must give of his soul; he must die. And in that death is man's rebirth.
>
> Looking into the mirror is a kind of death. It shows, not only our faces, but also the soul which illuminates the face. It reflects, not only the man who acts, but the actions of the man—both his deeds and his misdeeds, his love and his hate, his generosity and his cruelty. To see is to know, and to know is, on one level, to die. In the mirror, nothing is hidden, and there is virtue in the insight which is akin to wisdom. So just as this honesty kills, it also renews.

J.F.: THE ENDLESS MIRROR is unashamedly moralistic, which may be surprising when one learns that nearly all of the people (nearly sixty, in fact) who contributed material or who worked to put the book together are under twenty-five and supposedly uncommitted or cynical, according to popular stereotypes. Nor have we ferreted out the few remaining idealists for the project. We are a diverse group, from many different backgrounds, whose interests range from literature to computers. Some of the people are indeed very cynical and uncommitted about many things, but in the course of working together on THE ENDLESS MIRROR, they found their various perspectives merging on common ground: images of what should be, in contrast to an image of what is and has been. The images, as they are presented in the book, will seem complex or even chaotic, but that is the illusion we intend. In the mirror is a kaleidoscopic image of human experience, which cannot be simplified just to demonstrate underlying unities. We are very much concerned with truths and errors of human perceptions, which even we, the makers of this book, cannot avoid distorting. But as you come round and round to our recurring word/image patterns, we believe that the distortion factor lessens. No two people will read out the same message from each page or sequence, but ultimately the message pattern becomes definite, and we think convincing.

> *c.l.w.:* What should be is not necessarily different from what is or what has been. We have tried to be honest in our evaluation. We have tried to illustrate those elements in our being which are not what they should be, but correlatively, we have also indicated those positive elements which exist, and whose existence must be protected if man, as a species, is to survive.

> As a group we, who compiled this book, are extremely cynical. The pressures of twentieth-century existence have rendered us cautious. And it is this cynicism which is reflected in every page: Very few public illusions remain unexamined.

> Yet we are not entirely without hope—the book itself is a statement of that hope. If mankind has the ability to look into the mirror and to see Caliban without flinching from his duty to destroy the monster, then all is not lost.

> —And on the matter of distortion: Distortion is a deliberate critical approach used in the compilation of this book. We distort images, sometimes as society distorts, sometimes in a way unique to our own peculiar cynicism. In this sense, THE ENDLESS MIRROR is similar to the mirrors in a circus fun-house: It is calculated to reflect man and his society as grotesque. But in this grotesquerie man can see himself in all his multi-facets and can act upon the vision he sees.

J.F.: We contemplated providing neat, linear section headings for thematic sequences, but decided against it for the sake of avoiding compartmentalization of thought. The themes treated in THE ENDLESS MIRROR, both as ideas and as particular embodiments or variations of ideas, do interact, as we have said. But we would like to provide some kind of map for our book, so that the reader can better interpret its contents.

Many of the themes in THE ENDLESS MIRROR can be expressed as paradoxes or opposing statements:

> Time past has been lost, and we face an uncertain future.
> Time past and time future are embodied in the present: The past lives.

> Modern man is suspended death-like in life, without hope of rebirth.
> Death is the beginning of rebirth: We inherit the consciousness of our ancestors.

> The quest for truth and meaning is stalled in a web of illusions.
> The imaginative vision of experience is an illusion which dispels illusions.

> Lust for power and human exploitation grow at the expense of love.
> Love, in effacing self-interest, enlarges the self.

> Injustice, violence, and war reveal the absurdity of human destiny.
> Human survival depends not on self-protection, but on awareness of identity with Nature and the Environment.

> Vanity, pretense, and materialism ironically result in loneliness, isolation, or alienation.
> When the actors are unmasked, the first moment of horrified silence can turn to a moment of self-awareness, hitherto repressed.

> Woman, the Creator of our race, is ironically destroyed by objectification, idealization, and exploitation.
> In re-creating the Woman-Creator, we re-create the person, and ourselves.

> All people and things are different; yet they are the same.
> The sameness, when discovered, can change our identity from that of sheep to that of individual people.

> *c.l.w.:* Similarly, THE ENDLESS MIRROR is a sonata: theme, variation, theme. Sometimes it is difficult to isolate the theme, sometimes during compilation we lost sight of the theme entirely, but in retrospect our theme has evolved into an

assertion that man does exist, and that he is capable of both good and evil, and that man can will himself to choose the good over the evil if he is properly educated and critically self-analytical.

J.F.: The significance of the opposing statements above will grow fuller and clearer by the successive reinforcement of our pages. If some pages seem repetitious of what went before, look at the new surrounding context for new reflections, and consider how the impressions accumulate. We hope that by the end of the book (it does not really end—it just stops running), some of the very simple statements in word and image will carry weight because of the preparation made for them. It is no accident that in words we conclude, after the likes of Shakespeare, Hegel, and Wittgenstein, with a poem by a seventeen-year-old schoolgirl. We think that some more established poets who happen to see our book will wish that they had written that girl's poem. In her vision, a new cycle of life and imagination begins.

> *c.l.w.:* Life on our planet is an integrated system, which, like all systems, can become imbalanced as a whole if there is a tampering with the natural relationship of the parts. In an effort to reach the kind of harmonious equipoise which Renaissance idealists admired, man must come to an awareness of himself as one part of a cosmic whole, and in so doing he must learn to regard his every act in the perspective of the maintaining or destroying of the whole.

J.F.: Up to this point, we have presented a semblance of dialogue between two of the main participants in the project. Among other Friends who were also involved, Rande Mack, a student of literature, and Bobby Stifft, a graduate student in art, offer their perspectives on what kind of book we have made:

Rande Mack: THE ENDLESS MIRROR is an expression of reality—that reality which each person must face when he seeks to recognize himself in his role of living; that reality which our human history has generated; that reality which at once ignores and elevates our human instincts. The manuscript is built from quotations, photographs, and graphic art. These elements are arranged in such a way as to reflect a great many of the perspectives that man and woman have come to view themselves from. The material that forms these both obvious and obscure perspectives has been collected and constructed by us—men and women who as a group associated those reflections which we have noticed or created individually. We have attempted to relate images that would generate moods of different qualities. Just as many things are responsible for the perceptions of our individual and group existences, so too are many things at work in our book: tension, harmony, unity, discord, illusion, chaos, precision, insanity . . . The multicolored relationships between the images we have chosen are demonstrative of what we ourselves have perceived and learned. Reflected are not only the images and our reactions to them, but also our involvement in each other's reactions. We have recognized something more than ourselves, and we have called it THE ENDLESS MIRROR. This is a book which involves those who have fashioned it, those who have created the words and images in it, and those who will react to it.

Bobby Stifft: Being a graduate in art, I was intrigued from the first with the specific problems in relating words and graphics. Trying to juxtapose two languages, visual and written, so that they will play off one another has infinite possibilities. Since we were working within the context of a book, these were fortunately controlled by the major themes and overall intent. The format of a book itself offers a challenge: We have a history of written communication, set in type on rectangular white paper, with a left-to-right continuous narration as the accepted norm. Written words have their own specific kinds of time sequences, references, and sense stimuli, which play upon the eye, the reason, and the imagination. Incorporating *visual* language, with its own variety of communication and perception, compounds the problem of producing a coherent and creative whole. If one works individually, this type of problem resolves itself eventually in personal interests and limitations. Since THE ENDLESS MIRROR was a group effort, the interchange of materials and ideas enlarged both the scope and the limitations. Collaborative efforts, however, are extremely helpful in coming to a greater understanding of personal aims, while introducing new ways of thinking about and perceiving what one has already concluded upon, or even perhaps ignored.

J.F.: Finally, as general editor, I would like to make some acknowledgments. THE ENDLESS MIRROR could not have been done without the efforts of Ron Pogue in the coordination and production of photographic material. Endless ideas, intricate compilation, and countless hours were contributed by c.l. white. Elizabeth Bailey, carl coffman, and Sage Sigerson stayed with the project from the first with their help and contributions. Rande Mack, Mary Mongold, and Bobby Stifft joined us for the exhaustive revision of the original manuscript.

We are indebted to Montana State University and its affiliates for resources and material. In particular we are grateful to the Museum of the Rockies for its generous contribution of old photographs. We appreciate the cooperation of the Department of English and Theatre Arts, the Department of Film and Television, and the School of Art in the many facets of the project.

THE ENDLESS MIRROR was a Montana-based undertaking, but its effectiveness depends heavily upon New York: Thanks to Nick Ellison, our editor at Thomas Y. Crowell, who helped to initiate all of this in the first place, and who saw it through to completion. As rank amateurs in graphic layout and design, we were dependent upon the skill and imagination of the Crowell designers Judith Barry and Ingrid Beckman.

Boris Pasternak once observed that "in every generation there has to be some fool who will speak the truth as he sees it." For better or for worse, I guess that statement applies to our assemblage of mad, idealistic-cynical fools, but I will yield the floor to Walt Whitman, who wrote something in "Song of Myself" which encompasses many of our ideas and feelings:

Endless unfolding of words of ages!
And mine a word of the modern, the word En-Masse.
A word of the faith that never balks,
Here or henceforward it is all the same to me, I accept Time absolutely.

It alone is without flaw, it alone rounds and completes all,
That mystic baffling wonder alone completes all.

—JACK FOLSOM
Bozeman, Montana
February 1974

THE ENDLESS MIRROR
Jack Folsom & Friends

General Editor and Slave Driver: Jack Folsom
Text Editing and Coordination: c. l. white
   Assisted by: Elizabeth Bailey
Photographic Editing and Coordination: Ronald Pogue
   Assisted by: carl coffman
Graphic Art Coordination: Sage Sigerson
   Assisted by: Bobby Stifft
Permissions and Editorial Assistance: Rande Mack
                            Mary Mongold

Research and Development:

Barbara Becken	Robert Richardson
W. Kristelle Edgmond	Jim Ryan
Shelley Gaglia	Linda Schmiedeskamp
Dennis Lohof	Bruce Scoles
Will Makynen	Becky Stebbins
P. Carol Persons	Michael Wheat
Ellen Rawe	

Graphic Art Contributors:

Keith Anderson	Diane Pickering
Jeff Danforth	John Pollock
Dan De Voe	Jim Preston
Dennis De Weese	Ilmar Reinvald
Dianne Halverson	Sage Sigerson
Loren Kovich	Bobby Stifft
John R. Larson	Lanet Strobel
Phil Link	c. l. white
Richard Molander	

Photographic Contributors:

Barbara Becken
Robbie Berg
C. Kenneth Binkley
carl coffman
Lloyd Darrah
Ron Dobrowski
Joel Drubin
Peter Freivalds
Eric S. Hubbell
Paul Jesswein
Vicki Jorgenson
James Kautz
Kathy Krishna
Nancy Landgren

Michael J. LaValley
Michael J. Leaf
Dan Mongold
Mike Parent
Susan Peed
Ronald Pogue
David G. Rennie
Ken Slater
Bob Story
Jean Travis
Rebecca A. Widenhouse
Marty Wilcox
Dwain (Bill) Wolff

THE ENDLESS MIRROR

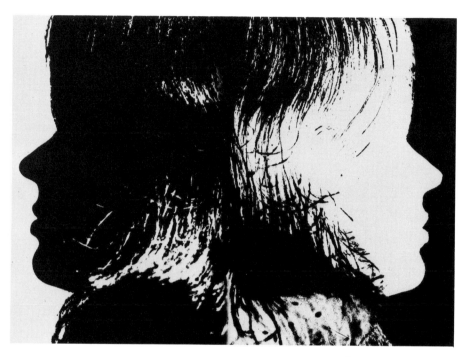

You, whom reverend love
   Made one another's hermitage;
You, to whom love was peace, that now is rage;
   Who did the whole world's soul extract, and drove
     Into the glasses of your eyes
     (So made such mirrors, and such spies,
That they did all to you epitomize)
   Countries, towns, courts: beg from above
   A pattern of your love!

        —JOHN DONNE, "The Canonization"

good morning

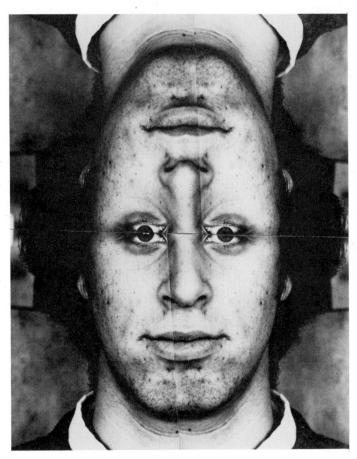

PHOTO BY JOEL DRUBIN

Every age is modern
to those who are living
in it.
—Benjamin Cardozo

The past went that-a-way. When faced with a totally new situation, we tend always to attach ourselves to the objects, to the flavor of the most recent past.... We look at the present through a rear view mirror. We march backwards into the future.

— MARSHALL McLUHAN

PHOTO BY RON POGUE

Baudelaire (1911)   BY RAYMOND DUCHAMP-VILLON

MIRRES VOUS Y
"BEHOLD YOURSELF THEREIN"

—JOHN SKELTON (1515)

SWIFT THE TIME

Child with his father
Watching the swirling waters from the riverbank
Wonders
Do I dare to jump in?
    Is it over my head?
    He asks
    Could I swim across by myself?
His father says, better not jump in
But then he says, yes
It's over your head, but you could get across
    And looking across
    The child has a memory
    Older than his father

And if, in the changing phases of man's life
I fall in sickness and in misery
my wrists seem broken and my heart seems dead
and strength is gone, and my life
is only the leavings of a life:

And still, among it all, snatches of lovely
oblivion, and snatches of renewal
odd, wintry flowers upon the withered stem,
yet new, strange flowers
such as my life has not brought forth before,
new blossoms of me.

—D. H. Lawrence, "Shadows"

PHOTO BY ERIC HUBBELL

SHORT THE LIFE

"The Public Places"

There was a child went forth every day,
And the first object he look'd upon, that object he became,

Diane Pickering

And that object became part of him for the day or a certain part of
  the day,
Or for many years or stretching cycles of years. . . .

            —Walt Whitman, "Autumn Rivulets"

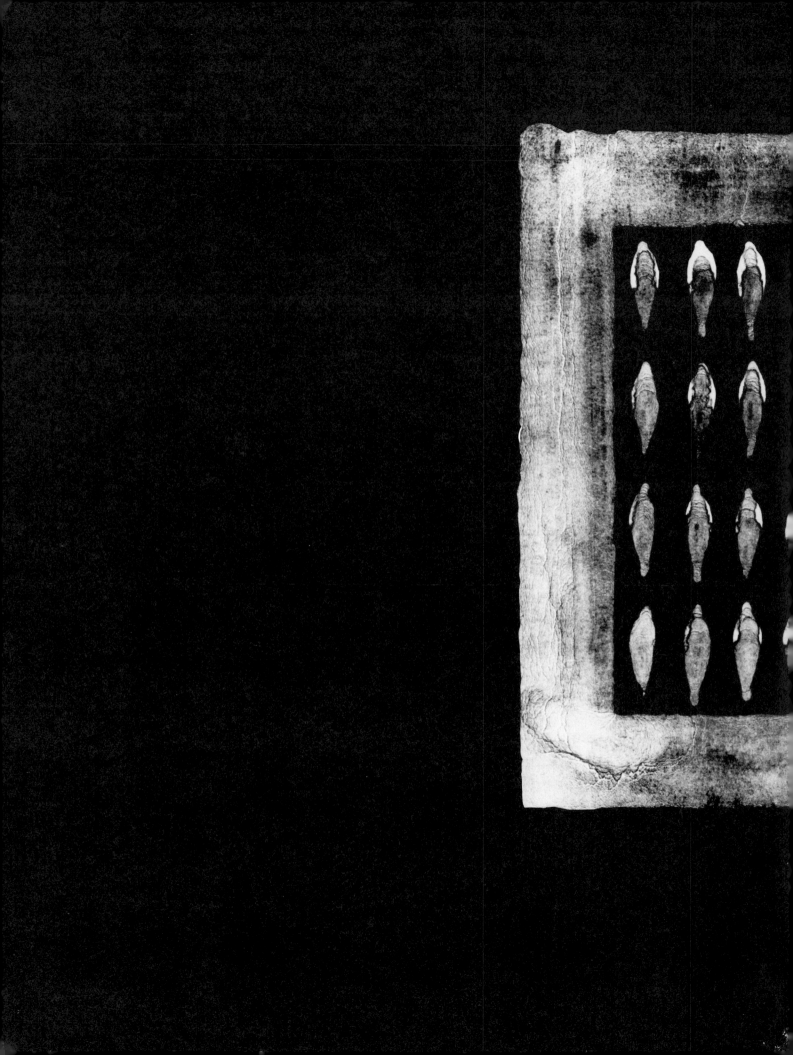

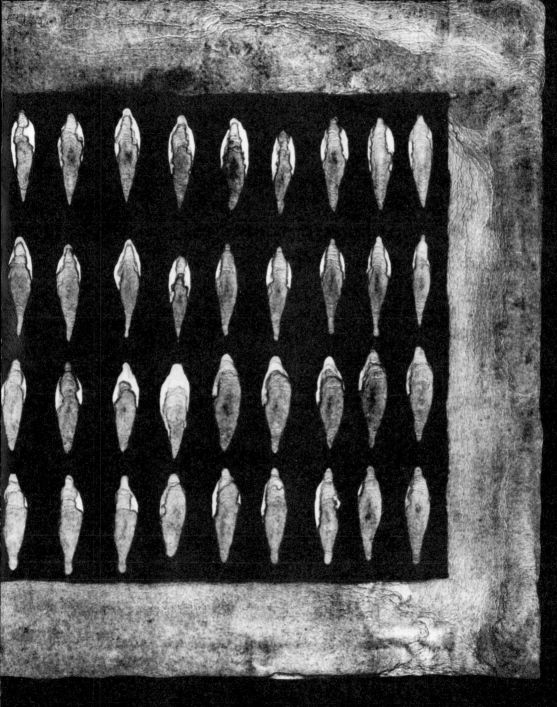

BY RICHARD MOLANDER

ONE MAN AND ONE
FLY BUZZING
TOGETHER IN A
SUNNY ROOM...
— ISSA

Evil I declare it and hostile to mankind—this document of the One, the Perfect, the Unmoved, the Sufficient, the Intransitory! The Intransitor—it is but a simile! And the poets lie exceedingly—but the best similes shall speak of time and becoming; they shall be for praise and justification of all transitoriness.

—FRIEDRICH NIETZSCHE, *Thus Spake Zarathustra*

DIALOGUE:
WHERE IS NOW?
WHAT IS REAL?

Beware that you do not lose the whole substance
by grasping at the shadow.

—AESOP

**To dismiss as non-existent what happens to be
indescribable is to equate existence with information.**

—LEWIS MUMFORD, *The Pentagon of Power*

Hippolyta: This is the silliest stuff that ever I heard.

Theseus: The best in this kind are but shadows; and the
worst are no worse if imagination amend them.

—WILLIAM SHAKESPEARE, *A Midsummer Night's Dream*

**I believe that the spiritual man must go back in order to
go forward. The way is circuitous, and sometimes lost,
but invariably returned to.**

—THEODORE ROETHKE, *On the Poet and His Craft*

HE COULD BE RIGHT

A dream itself is but a shadow.

—William Shakespeare, *Hamlet*

"The Transformation of Cornelius Cheevers"   Loren Kovich

"Mars and Venus United by Love"   PAOLO VERONESE

And in this fatall mirrour of transgression,
Shewes man as fruit of his degeneration,
The errours ugly infinite impression,
Which beares the faithless downe to desperation . . . .

—FULKE GREVILLE, *Caelica* XCIX

"*I WILL SPEAK IN MY OWN DEFENSE!*"

— BOBBY SEALE

"You have the floor—explain yourself—
you are free" (1835)

HONORÉ DAUMIER

"Congratulations, Baer—I think you've wiped out the species!"

[18]

PHOTO BY RON POGUE

PHOTOS BY RON POGUE

SIMPLIFY

IT'S A LOT

Covering the earth with odours, fruits, and flocks,
Thronging the Seas with spawn innumerable . . . .

—JOHN MILTON, *Comus*

PHOTO BY DAVE RENNIE

In winter, when the fields are white,
    I sing this song for your delight—
In spring, when woods are getting green,
    I'll try and tell you what I mean.
In summer, when the days are long,
    Perhaps you'll understand the song.
In autumn, when the leaves are brown,
    Take pen and ink, and write it down.

—LEWIS CARROLL, *Through the Looking Glass*

[22]

. . . The selfishness of selfishness is the reluctance to be born.

—NORMAN O. BROWN, *Love's Body*

To ask a child to be unselfish is wrong. Every child is an egotist, and the world belongs to him.

—A. S. NEILL, *Summerhill*

It's okay to argue with the teacher

I am of old and young, of foolish as much as the wise,
Regardless of others, ever regardful of others,
Maternal as well as paternal, a child as well as a man. . . .

—WALT WHITMAN, "Song of Myself"

Dieu est un enfant qui s'amuse,
Passe du rire aux larmes sans motifs et invent chaque jour le monde.

—ÉLIE FAURE

INSIDE THE CURTAIN . . . A MIND LOOKING OUT OUTSIDE . . . A WORLD LOOKING IN

PHOTO BY BILL WOLFF

There is nothing behind the curtain other than that
which is in front of it.

—Georg Wilhelm Friedrich Hegel

In a world in which one is essentially and ever alone, it is a relief to confront the existence of one's shadow; to gaze out at night seeking the eyes of another who is seeking one's own and know that in some way there has been a meaningful exchange; to sense that somehow on the transversal of time, aloneness is banished if only for an instant and that one thereby has touched the threshold of the eternal. What opens the door to the beyond is the recognition that the stranger is one's self.

—C. L. WHITE

"Contrariwise," continued Tweedledee,
"If it was so, it might be; and if it were so, it would be—
But as it isn't, it ain't, that's logic."

—Lewis Carroll

" . . . DO I CONTRADICT MYSELF?"

—Walt Whitman

[31]

"Diane"   by Judith Woracek Barry

CONTRARIWISE ...

"Proof 2" (1969)   JIM PRESTON

. . . Despite the historians, there has been only one age of man. It is the age of primitive man. The beginning of the age of civilized man, when it comes, will be marked by political, philosophical, and spiritual awareness of himself as a member of a world species with world needs and with the capacity and desire to create world institutions to meet these needs. Humankind need not sacrifice the nation to create such institutions. It need only recognize and assert an allegiance of humans to one another beyond national boundaries and to do those things in the human interest that the nation as an organization is capable of doing.

The present mode of life on earth is madness, which is nonetheless lethal for being legal. Rational existence is possible, but it calls for a world consciousness and a world design. People who develop the habit of thinking of themselves as world citizens are fulfilling the first requirement of sanity in our time.

—NORMAN COUSINS, "Amchitka and Tribalism," an editorial in *The Saturday Review*, Sept. 25, 1971, p. 30

The problem with

"We take our jolly good time."

JAMES GILLRAY (1795)

Who speaks of conquering? To endure is everything.

—RAINER MARIA RILKE

Are there not thousands in the world . . .
Who love their fellows even to the death,
And feel the giant agony of the world . . . ?

—JOHN KEATS

GRACE FOR LOVE

Ah
Power that swirls us
Together
Grant us bliss
Grant us the
      Great Release

And to all Beings
Vanishing,
Wounded,
In trouble on Earth
We give of our love
May their numbers
Increase
                — Gary Snyder

"Propithecus Verreauxi Coronatus"

ALFRED GRANDIDIER (Madagascar, 1866)

The mind is its own place, and in itself
Can make a Heaven of Hell, a Hell of Heaven . . . .

—JOHN MILTON, *Paradise Lost*

"Encounter"   M C. ESCHER

Not until the creation and maintenance of decent conditions of life for
all men are recognized and accepted as a common obligation of all men
. . . shall we be able to speak of mankind as civilized.

—ALBERT EINSTEIN

"...TO SPEAK OF MANKIND AS CIVILIZED."

The first man, who, having enclosed a piece of ground, bethought himself of saying, "This is mine," and found people simple enough to believe him, was the real founder of our society.

—Jean Jacques Rousseau

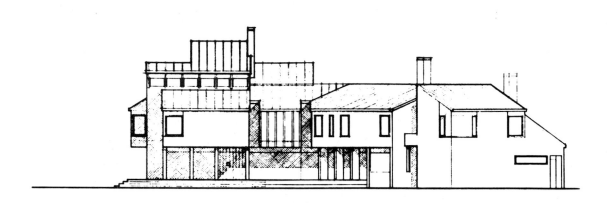

EAST ELEVATION

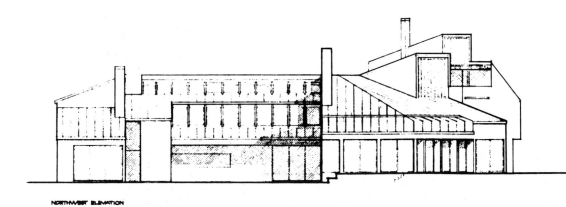

NORTHWEST ELEVATION

ARCHITECTURAL RENDERING BY ILMAR REINVALD

THIS IS MINE

PHOTO BY DAN MONGOLD

burly was never seen since the Devil was a little Boy; and there will be above seven and twenty irregular Verbs made this Year, if Priscian don't hold them in. If God don't help us, we shall have our hands and hearts full. But on the other side, if He be with us, nothing can hurt us, as says the Celestial Star-gazer, who was wrapt into the Third Heaven, Rom. the 7th; *Si Deus pro nobis quis contra nos?* If God be with us, who will be against us? In good faith, *Nemo domine;* No body, an 't like your Worship; for He is as Powerful as He is Good. Here for the same, praise ye his Holy Name.

CHAPTER III

Of the Diseases this Year

THIS Year the Stone-blind shall see but very little; the Deaf shall hear but scurvily; the Dumb shan't speak very plain; the Rich shall be somewhat in a better case than the Poor, and the Healthy than the Sick. Whole Flocks, Herds, and Droves of Sheep, Swine, and Oxen; Cocks and Hens, Ducks and Drakes, Geese and Ganders, shall go to Pot; but the Mortality will not be altogether so great among Apes, Monkeys, Baboons, and Dromedaries. As for old Age, 'twill be incurable this Year, because of the Years past. Those who are sick of the Pleurisy, will feel a plaguy Stitch in their Sides; those who are troubled with the Thoro'-go-nimble or Wild-squirt, will often prostitute their Blind-cheeks to the Bog-house. Catarrhs this Year shall distill from the Brain on the lower Parts; Sore Eyes will by no means help the Sight; Ears shall be at least as scarce and short in Gascony, and among Knights of the Post, as ever: A most horrid and dreadful, virulent, malignant, catching, perverse, and odious Malady, shall be almost Epidemical, insomuch that many shall run mad upon 't, not knowing what Nail to drive to keep the Wolf from the Door, very often plotting, contriving, cudgelling, and puzling their weak, shallow Brains, and syllogiz-ing and prying up and down for the Philosopher's-Stone, tho' they only get Midas's Lugs by the bargain. I quake for very fear when I think on 't; for I assure you, few will escape this Disease, which Averoes calls Lack of Money: And by Conse-quence of the last Year's Comet, and Saturn's Retrogradation, a huge drivelling He-Scoundrel, all be-crinkum'd and colly-flower'd shall die in the Spittle ; at his Death will be a horrid clutter between the Cats and the Rats, Hounds and Hares, Hawks and Ducks, and eke between the Monks and Eggs.

CHAPTER IV

Of the Fruits of the Earth this Year

I FIND by the Calculations of Albumazar, in his Book of the great Conjunction, and elsewhere, That this will be a plentiful Year of all manner of good things to those that have enough ; but your Hops of Picardy will go near to fare the worse for the Cold. As for Oates, they 'll be a great help to Horses. I dare say, there won't be much more Bacon than Swine : Pisces having the Ascendant, 'twill be a mighty Year for Muscles, Cockles, and Perrywinkles. Mercury somewhat threatens our Parsly-beds, yet Parsly will be to be had for Money. Hemp will grow faster than the Children of this Age, and some will find there 's but too much on 't. There will be but a very few Bon-Christians, but Choak-pears in abundance. As for Corn, Wine, Fruit, and Herbs, there never was such Plenty as will be now, if poor Folks have their wish.

CHAPTER V

Of the Disposition of the People this Year

'TIS the oddest Whimsy in the World, to fansie there are Stars for Kings, Popes, and Great Dons, any more than for the Poor and Needy. As if, forsooth, some new Stars were made since the Flood, or since Romulus or Pharamond, at the making some body King : A thing that Triboulet or Caillette would have been asham'd to have said, and yet they were Men of no common Learning or Fame ; and, for ought you or I know, this same Triboulet may have been of the Kings of Castille's Blood in Noah's Ark, and Caillette of that of King Priam. Now, mark

We knowers are unknown to ourselves, and for a
good reason: how can we hope to find what we have
never looked for? There is a sound adage that runs:
"Where a man's treasure lies, there lies his heart."
Our treasure lies in the beehives of our knowledge.
We are perpetually on our way thither, being by
nature winged insects and honey gatherers of the
mind. The only thing that lies close to our heart is
the desire to bring something home to the hive. As
for the rest of life—so-called "experience"—who
among us is serious enough for that? Or has time
enough? When it comes to such matters, our heart is
simply not in it—we don't even lend our ear.

—FRIEDRICH NIETZSCHE, *The Genealogy of Morals*

Our friends float past; we become involved with them; they float on, and we must rely on hearsay or lose track of them completely; they float back again, and we must either renew our friendship—catch up to date—or find that they and we don't comprehend each other any more.

—JOHN BARTH, *The Floating Opera*

The terminology of the question

determines the terminology of the answer.

—WENDELL JOHNSON, *People in Quandaries*

This nation . . . a place where the meaning of man's life matches the marvels of man's labor.

—LYNDON B. JOHNSON

[44]

DELLA
N MAY 14, 1875
D JAN. 16, 1913

MES C.
RICKARD

MARY C.
BLILER
BORN
FEB 7, 1855

BLILER

ROSANA
RICKARD
10. 10. 1842
8. 9. 1913
GONE HOME

[45]

"The obvious is better than obvious avoidance of it."—H. W. Fowler. "Peace and Justice are two sides of the same coin."—Dwight D. Eisenhower. "Two dangers constantly threaten the world: order and disorder."—Paul Valéry. "Man is nature's sole mistake."—Alexander Pope. "If you want to get to plain truth, do not be concerned with right and wrong. The conflict between right and wrong is the sickness of the mind."—the *Hsin-hsin Ming.* "We believe whatever we want to believe."—Demosthenes. "Actions speak louder than words, but not as often." "A man is born to hereditary rank; or his being appointed to certain office gives him a certain rank. Subordination tends greatly to human happiness. Were we all upon an equality, we should have no other enjoyment than mere animal pleasure."—Samuel Johnson. "One can only abuse the things which are good."—Michel Eyquem de Montaigne.

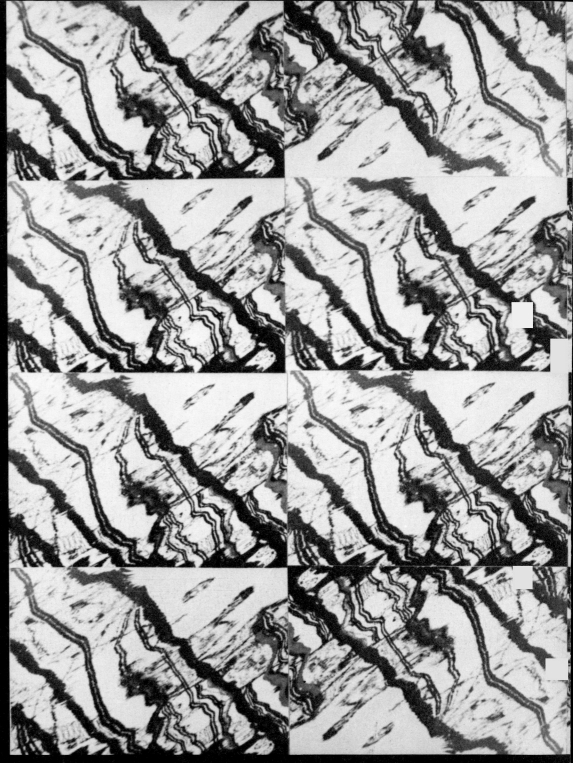

PHOTO BY KEN SLATER

FACED WITH INFORMATION OVER

[50]

I used to think that anyone doing anything weird was weird.
I suddenly realized that anyone doing anything weird wasn't weird at
all and that it was the people saying they were weird that were weird.

—PAUL McCARTNEY

WEIRD?

If anyone seeing a player acting his part on a stage should go about to strip him of his disguise and show him to the people in his true native form, would he not, think you, not only spoil the whole design of the play, but deserve himself to be pelted off with stones as a phantastical fool and one out of his wits? But nothing is more common with them than such changes; the same person one while impersonating a woman, and another while a man; now a youngster, and by and by a grim seignior; now a king, and presently a peasant; now a god, and in a trice again an ordinary fellow. But to discover this were to spoil all, it being the only thing that entertains the eyes of the spectators. And what is all this life but a kind of comedy, wherein men walk up and down in one another's disguises and act their respective parts, till the property-man brings them back to the attiring house. And yet he often orders a different dress, and makes him that came but just now off in the robes of a king put on the rags of a beggar. Thus are all things represented by counterfeit, and yet without this there was no living.

—ERASMUS, *The Praise of Folly* (1509)

"Pie-Eating Contest"

Life comes in a thousand shades of gray, and everyone except madmen
think what they do is reasonable, and maybe even madmen do too.

—JOHN D. MACDONALD, *A Deadly Shade of Gold*

WE ENCOUNTER
REMOTE
PREDECESSORS

DELEIGHTFUL PIE

the fat man eats pie. he eats pie this way
first he takes a small bite with his fork
then he takes a larger piece and smells it
with his nose, then he places nose and mouth
close to the plate and he eats deleightful
pie quick quick quick someone is watching

DELEIGHTFUL PIE

Once upon a time, once upon a time there was a man, who must have been a magic man, there
was a man who ate pie. He ate custard pie and lemon pie and apple pie and coconut pie and
mince pie and pumpkin pie and rhubarb pie and cherry pie and whatever other kind of pie a
person can think of. Now, you might ask, what is so special about a man who eats pie, what is so
magical about a man who eats ordinary pie? Now, that's an altogether fair question. It is also a
question which is answerable. And the answer is this tale, for it isn't, of course, WHAT one eats
that is important, but what IS important is HOW one eats what one eats.

Now this man, this marvellous pie eater, this magical special man, was also, as we say, an
important-man-in-the-world. He was important not because he ate pie of course, for anyone
can eat pie, even, after all, a person without teeth can eat pie after all. So eating pie in itself is
not that special. He was an important-man-in-the-world because he WAS that way, a natural
characteristic, like the size of one's nose. He just was, this pie eater, an important-man-in-the-
world. So.

One day, it was mid-afternoon of a bright clear blue high cloud and light wind from the
southwest day, typical of the kind of day we have in the midwest in late August, well, on this
day, the man was in a building by the river where food was served. He took a piece of pie from
the counter and placed it carefully on his tray. Now this act alone took some time. For first the
man watched each piece of pie for a good long solid time. Looked at each piece closely and
attentively, the way kids look at weeds and things to see if they can actually see them grow. He
watched the pies that way. He stared, for example, at the pecan pie, almost as long as a worm
stares at the full moon. (And you know how long that is!) When he had stared at each possible
piece of pie that way, he drew back from the counter, heaved a great sigh, threw his eyes into
the air, and then, quite suddenly, his fat chop of a hand leaped out of his body and seized a
piece of coconut cream pie. Seized, that is, the plate on which the pie sat. When the pie in its
plate was on the man's tray he watched it again for a while, almost unhappily. One can never
know another person completely, so that we can only guess just exactly why the magic pie eater
MAY have been slightly unhappy at this point. All one can safely say is that our important
man seemed unhappy, at least for the moment.

Then the man walked to the milk dispenser, drew himself a glass, a tall chalky white glass, of
good pure whole 100% milk from an all-American cow. He drew it PROUDLY, as an
American salutes the flag proudly, or thinks proudly of all the wars we have won as a nation.
He held the glass before him as a proud soldier holds his rifle before him for the inspecting
officer to inspect. Then he put it carefully on his tray beside the pie and walked to the cashier.
He paid for the milk and pie, holding his head down, as if he didn't want the cashier to
recognize him, as if he wanted to be the incognito pie eater, the one who traveled fartherest
Mexico in his mini-bus, eating pie all over the Yucatán Peninsula in dark glasses and no name.
So that when the cashier said thank you, he didn't even want her to hear his voice. And so he

took his change and glided, or glid, like a spoon-snake, to his familiar table by the tall pillar overlooking the moving waters of the ribber.

There he placed his tray on the table and sat down. Now he put both hands on the table and stared for just a bit at the moving waters, just as long as it takes to run through a prayer, or count from one to ten, if one counts quickly. Then he took a fork and poised it over the pie. Then, scooping a small piece he raised it to his nose, just a second or two off his thick dragondroopy mustachios, and inhaled, as if the pie were or was some heavenly scented flower. Satisfied with whatever he smelled, he returned the piece of pie to the plate and commenced to look furtively about to see if he was being watched. He looked left and right and up and down. After all, what kind of pie eater is it that could eat pie while being watched? I ask you. What, I want to know, is your answer, eh? Well, feeling all safe and secure, our important man patted his mustache with his right forefinger, adjusted his glasses with his left thumb and index finger, gazed furtively and secretively about once again, then took, slowly, a bit of a drink of that 100% milk. Next he took both hands and pulled his sweater down over his belly. It was a large capacious wonderful sort of clown belly. It was, in a word, important.

Then, eyes shifting left and right and up and down, he drew his mouth close to the plate and quick quick quick he shovelled and scooped and forked the pie into the opening below his nose that we usually call the mouth. Ah, ah! quick quick quick, someone is watching! Ah! Such deleightful pie!

Now the pie was gone. Our man sat back in his chair and stared at the moving waters while drinking the rest of his milk. Again there was a sadness on his face, as if someone he loved very much had left for Dubuque, or Wappello. Or as if he was expecting something very strange to happen. The waters moved and rushed and churned before his eyes. Then a tear came to his eye, perhaps a tear for all the lost pies, er that is, lost people, I mean peeple, all those lost in the floods and so forth. Well, we can never know. Then our man rose, placed his two hands on his belly, and was gone.

—George Chambers

The Sleepers

I wander all night in my vision,
Stepping with light feet, swiftly and noiselessly stepping and stopping,
Bending with open eyes over the shut eyes of sleepers,
Wandering and confused, lost to myself, ill-assorted, contradictory,
Pausing, gazing, bending, and stopping.

How solemn they look there, stretch'd and still,
How quiet they breathe, the little children in their cradles.

The wretched features of ennuyés, the white features of corpses, the livid faces of drunkards,
the sick-gray faces of onanists,
The gash'd bodies on battle-fields, the insane in their strong door'd rooms, the sacred idiots,
the new-born emerging from gates, and the dying emerging from gates,
The night pervades them and infolds them.

The married couple sleep calmly in their bed, he with his palm on the hip of the wife, and
she with her palm on the hip of her husband,
The sisters sleep lovingly side by side in their bed,
The men sleep lovingly side by side in theirs,
And the mother sleeps with her little child carefully wrapt.

The blind sleep, and the deaf and dumb sleep,
The prisoner sleeps well in the prison, the runaway son sleeps,
The murderer that is to be hung next day, how does he sleep?
And the murder'd person, how does he sleep?

The female that loves unrequited sleeps,
And the male that loves unrequited sleeps,
The head of the money-maker that plotted all day sleeps,
And the enraged and treacherous dispositions, all, all sleep.

I stand in the dark with drooping eyes by the worst-suffering and the most restless,
I pass my hands soothingly to and fro a few inches from them,
The restless sink in their beds, they fitfully sleep.

Now I pierce the darkness, new beings appear,
The earth recedes from me into the night,
I saw that it was beautiful, and I see that what is not the earth is beautiful.

I go from bedside to bedside, I sleep close with the other sleepers each in turn,
I dream in my dream all the dreams of the other dreamers,
And I become the other dreamers. . . .

—WALT WHITMAN

"Sleepers, II" (1959)   GEORGE TOOKER

Glimpse of the Ice

I am sure now
A light under the skin coming nearer
Bringing snow
Then at nightfall a moth has thawed out and is
Dripping against the glass
I wonder if death will be silent after all
Or a cry frozen in another age

—W. S. MERWIN

"La Comida Frugal" (The Frugal Repast), 1904

PABLO PICASSO

[58]

journey
to infinity

NEVER, NEVER, NEVER, NEVER, NEVER . . .

—WILLIAM SHAKESPEARE

Over the music he screams into my ear.
He asks how old I am   asks if I am married
He says not to   ever. He says he loves
his wife and kids but that there are times
such as tonight   when   they don't get along.
        he stops
    the music stops
He leans over a Gin and Tonic
stares into it as if he were looking
    for a prophecy
His nods keep time
    as the music starts

—WILL MAKYNEN

Morning

Up at dawn today with
The kids. Made pancakes
again.

Went to the doctor —
need dentures!!! Afraid
to tell George!

Lunch

I tore some of my
hair out by the roots in
the new electric rollers!!

Afternoon

Watched a romantic
movie on TV — George
fell asleep at the end
of it...

Evening

Death is the mother of beauty;
    Hence from her
Alone, shall come fulfillment
    To our dreams
And our desires.

—WALLACE STEVENS, "Sunday Morning"

"Head of A Woman"

In a society without sex repression, the unmentionable would disappear. Being shocked implies having an obscene interest in what shocks you.

—A. S. Neill, *Summerhill*

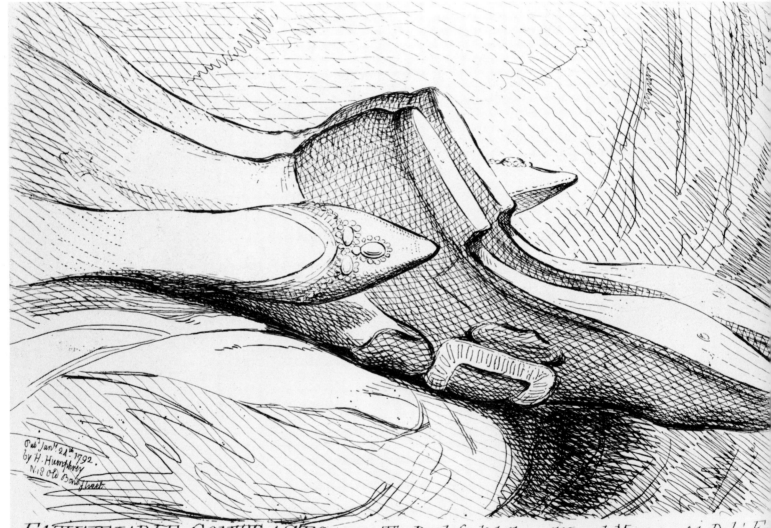

FASHIONABLE CONTRASTS;—or—*The Duchess's little Shoe yeilding to the Magnitude of the Duke's Foo*

JAMES GILLRAY (1792)

Show and tell

Nature has placed mankind under the governance of two sovereign masters, pain and pleasure.

It is for them alone to point out what we ought to do, as well as to determine what we shall do . . . . They govern us in all we do, in all we say, in all we think: every effort we can make to throw off our subjection, will serve but to demonstate and confirm it.

—Jeremy Bentham

HER SCOLDING WAS BUT IN VAIN

To be great is to be misunderstood.
—Ralph Waldo Emerson

In euery daunse, of a moste auncient custome, there daunseth to gether a man and a woman, holding eche other by the hande or the arme, which betokeneth concorde.

—Sir Thomas Elyot, *The Boke named the Gouvernour* (1531)

What are you waiting for?

We are so accustomed to disguising ourselves from others, that we end by disguising ourselves from ourselves.

—Duc François de La Rochefoucauld

Listen to what you've been missing

WOMEN LOVE MEN

I care not for these ladies
That must be wood and pride,
Give me kind Amarillis
The wanton country maid;
Nature art *disdaineth*,
Her beauty is her own;

Her when we court and kiss,
She cries *forsooth*, let go.
But when we come where comfort is
She never will say no.

—Thomas Campion (1597–1620)

H O T

AESTAS.
IVNIVS AVGVSTVS, MATVRIS IVLIVS ARVIS
AESTATEM, MESSES SOLE COQVENTE, FACIT

P. Cand. pinxit. C. G. ab Amling delin. et sculpsit. 1699.

THE HEAT OF SUMMER

You emerge into another world inside the woman.

—NORMAN O. BROWN, *Love's Body*

PHOTOS BY KEN SLATER

There is no mockery between women. One lies down at peace as at one's own breast.

—ANAÏS NIN, *House of Incest*

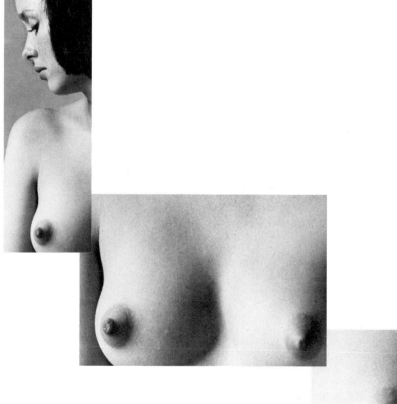

PHOTOS BY RON POGUE

Woman is woman's natural ally.

—EURIPIDES, *Alope*

Our liberties, our lives, are in danger.

—Cato (63 b.c.)

my mind misgives
Some consequence yet hanging in the stars
Shall bitterly begin his fearful date
With this night's revels.

—William Shakespeare, *Romeo and Juliet*

Our only hope is that sooner or later our whole society gets so plastic that we can throw it out.

—MASON WILLIAMS, *The FCC Rapport*

In every organism, individual or social,
there is a tendency amounting at times
to a voluptuous desire, to let go of
the present which is always innovation
     and to fall back out of sheer inertia
       into that which is past and habitual;
a tendency to make itself
            gradually archaic.

—José Ortega y Gasset

The Times They Are A'Changin'

Come gather 'round people wherever you roam
And admit that the waters around you have grown
And accept it that soon you'll be drenched to the bone.
If your time to you is worth savin'
Then you'd better start swimmin' or you'll sink like a stone,
For the times they are a'changin'.

Come writers and critics who prophesy with your pen,
And keep your eyes wide; the chance won't come again.
And don't speak too soon for the wheel's still in spin,
And there's no tellin' who that it's namin'.
For the loser now will be later to win,
For the times they are a'changin'.

Come mothers and fathers throughout the land
And don't criticize what you can't understand.
Your sons and your daughters are beyond your command
And your old world is rapidly agin'.
Please get out of the new one if you can't lend a hand,
For the times they are a'changin'.

Come senators, congressmen, please heed the call.
Don't stand in the doorway; don't block up the hall.
For he who gets hurt will be he who has stalled.
There's a battle outside and it's ragin'.
It will soon shake your windows and rattle your walls,
For the times they are a'changin'.

The line it is drawn; the curse it is cast.
The slow one now will later be fast.
As the present now will later be past.
The order is rapidly fadin'.
And the first one now will later be last.
For the times they are a'changin'.

—Bob Dylan

"The System Investigates Itself" (1921)   BOARDMAN ROBINSON

It is said that when the Bishop of Worcester returned from the Oxford meeting of the British Association in 1860, he informed his wife, at tea, that the horrid Professor Huxley had declared that man was descended from the apes. Whereupon the dear lady is said to have exclaimed, "Descended from the apes! Let us hope that it is not true, but if it is true, let us pray that it will not become generally known."

—S. A. BARNETT, "On the Hazards of Analogies"

TIMES ARE
A'CHANGIN'?

"Portrait of James Loper" (1952)   ANDREW WYETH

Amherst College Collection; courtesy Amherst Department of Fine Arts

Bitten by fleas and lice,
I slept in a bed,
A horse urinating all the time
Close to my pillow.

—BASHO (1644–1694)

These are the voices which we hear in solitude, but they grow faint and inaudible when we enter into the world. Society everywhere is in conspiracy against the manhood of every one of its members. Society is a joint-stock company, in which the members agree, for the better securing of his bread to each shareholder, to surrender the liberty and culture of the eater. The virtue in most request is conformity. Self-reliance is its aversion. It loves not realities and creators, but names and customs.

Whoso would be a man, must be a nonconformist. He who would gather immortal palms must not be hindered by the name of goodness, but must explore if it be goodness. Nothing is at last sacred but the integrity of your own mind.

—RALPH WALDO EMERSON, "Self-Reliance"

Courtesy, Museum of Fine Arts, Boston; gift by contribution

Portrait bust of a Roman

DRAWINGS BY SAGE SIGERSON

Truth will not afford sufficient food to their vanity; so they have betaken themselves to errour. Truth, Sir, is a cow which will yield such people no more milk, and so they are gone to milk the bull.

—SAMUEL JOHNSON

[75]

BY RICHARD MOLANDER

COSMOGRAPHY

Behold the world, how it is whirled round,
And for it is so whirl'd, is named so;
In whose large volume many rules are found
Of this new art, which it doth fairly show;
For your quick eyes in wand'ring to and fro,
    From east to west, on no one thing can glance,
    But if you mark it well, it seems to dance. . . .

For, lo, the sea that fleets about the land
And like a girdle clips her solid waist,
Music and measure both doth understand;
For his great crystal eye is always cast
Up to the moon, and on her fixed fast,
    And as she danceth in her pallid sphere
    So danceth he about the center here. . . .

—SIR JOHN DAVIES, *Orchestra* (1596)

DELINEATIO PRÆLY NAVALIS, INTER VENETOS ET TURCAS DIE 24.25.et26. IUNY ANN. 1656. ad Dardanellos in Morea acerrimé commiss: Venetis insignem Victoriam reportantibus.

Abbildung deß denckwürdigen See Treffens, zwischen den Venetianern vnd Türcken, bey den beyden Castellen in Morea Dardanelli genannt, den 24. 25. vnd 26. Juny dieses 1656. Jahrs vorgangen: worinnen die Venetianer einen gantz Herrlichen Sieg erhalten.

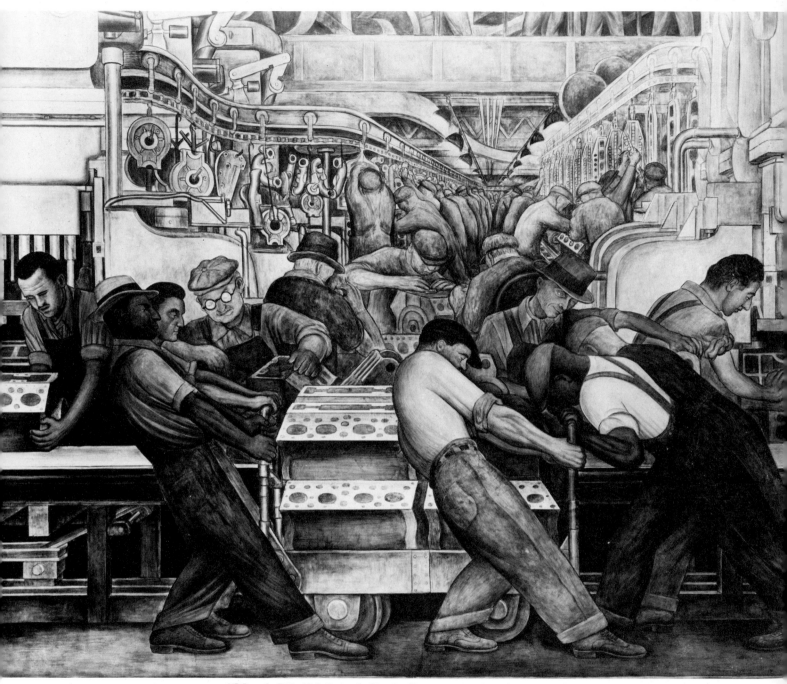

"North Wall Mural: Body Presses and Assembly"   DIEGO RIVERA

No one knows what he can't do until he tries.

What immense innovations are being wrought all around us now . . .
how can artists portray it all with the old means of art?

—Bertolt Brecht

PHOTO BY PAUL JESSWEIN

[81]

Insanity in individuals is something rare—but in groups, parties, nations and epochs it is the rule.

—FRIEDRICH NIETZSCHE

War is no longer an interruption of peace; in fact, peace itself has become an uneasy interlude between wars; peace has become a perilous balance of mutual terror and mutual fright.

—C. WRIGHT MILLS, *The Causes of World War III*

"WAR
AND MAMMON
ARE THE SAME"

"Combat of the Tire-Lires [moneybags] and the Coffre-forts [strong-boxes]," sixteenth century

ENGRAVING AFTER BRUEGHEL

[83]

If a European, when he has cut off his beard, and put false hair on his head, or bound up his own natural hair in regular hard knots, as unlike nature as he can possibly make it . . . meets a Cherokee Indian, who has . . . laid on with equal care and attention his yellow and red ocher on particular parts of his forehead and cheeks . . . whoever of these two despises the other for this attention to the fashion of his country, whichever first feels himself provoked to laugh, is the barbarian.

—William Blake's Annotations
to Joshua Reynolds' *Discourses*
(1808 edition)

Kunsthistorisches Museum, Vienna

"Emperor Maximilian I" (1509)

<small></small>Jörg Muscat

WHO IS THE
BARBARIAN?

Chad MacKenzie as "The Crier" in *Masque of the Absorakee*

The mind does everything, for there is nothing but the mind. The mind creates and destroys and commands. You do not control your mind, but It often lets you think you do.

"Fit for Active Service" (1916–17),

pen and brush and India ink, 20 x 14 3/8"

GEORGE GROSZ

"Card Players"   C. Owen Smithers

Let us affront and reprimand the smooth mediocrity and squalid contentment of the times, and hurl in the face of custom, and trade, and office, the fact which is the upshot of all history, that there is a great responsible Thinker and Actor working wherever a man works; that a true man belongs to no other time or place, but is the centre of things. Where he is, there is nature. . . . Every true man is a cause, a country, and an age; requires infinite spaces and numbers and time fully to accomplish his design.

—Ralph Waldo Emerson, "Self-Reliance"

. . . everyone around me is so false
that I'm constantly lowering my ideals.

—Happy, *Death of a Salesman*
by ARTHUR MILLER

There must be a GOD and he can't know Anything About US

As flies to wanton boys, are we to th' gods,
They kill us for their sport.

—WILLIAM SHAKESPEARE, *King Lear*

THE BOOK OF JOB

CHAPTER 7: Job excuseth his desire of death. He complaineth
of his own restlessness, and God's watchfulness.

Is there not an appointed time to man upon earth? Are not his days also like the days of an hireling? As a servant earnestly desireth the shadow, and as an hireling looketh for the reward of his work: so am I made to possess months of vanity, and wearisome nights are appointed to me. When I lie down, I say, When shall I arise, and the night be gone? and I am full of tossings to and fro unto the dawning of the day. My flesh is clothed with worms and clods of dust; my skin is broken, and become loathsome. My days are swifter than a weaver's shuttle, and are spent without hope. O remember that my life is wind: mine eye shall no more see good. The eye of him that hath seen me shall see me no more: thine eyes are upon me, and I am not. As the cloud is consumed and vanisheth away: so he that goeth down to the grave shall come up no more. Therefore I will not refrain my mouth; I will speak in the anguish of my spirit; I will complain in the bitterness of my soul.

Am I a sea, or a whale, that thou settest a watch over me? When I say, My bed shall comfort me, my couch shall ease my complaint; then thou scarest me with dreams, and terrifiest me through visions: so that my soul chooseth strangling, and death rather than my life. I loathe it; I would not live alway: let me alone; for my days are vanity.

What is man, that thou shouldest magnify him? and that thou shouldest set thine heart upon him? and that thou shouldest visit him every morning, and try him every moment? How long wilt thou not depart from me, nor let me alone till I swallow down my spittle? I have sinned; what shall I do unto thee, O thou preserver of men? Why hast thou set me as a mark against thee, so that I am a burden to myself? And why dost thou not pardon my transgression, and take away mine iniquity?

For now shall I sleep in the dust: and thou shalt seek me in the morning, but I shall not be.

CHAPTER 8:

Then answered Bildad the Shuhite, and said:

. . . Though thy beginning was small, yet thy latter end should greatly increase. For enquire, I pray thee, of the former age, and prepare thyself to the search of their fathers.

For we are but of yesterday, and know nothing, because our days upon earth are a shadow. . . .

"Hand with Reflecting Globe"   M. C. ESCHER

Economy

No need to break the mirror.
Here is the face shattered,
Good for seven years of sorrow.

—W. S. MERWIN

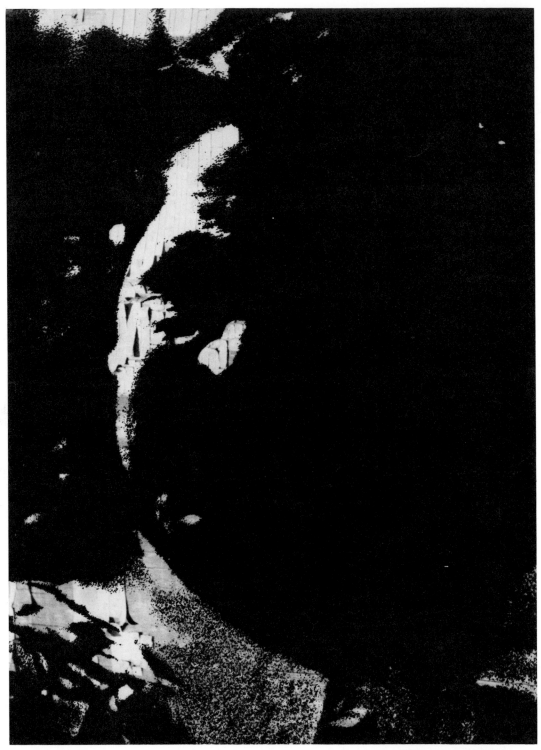

The world too is an illusion composed of everything ever thought or dreamed.

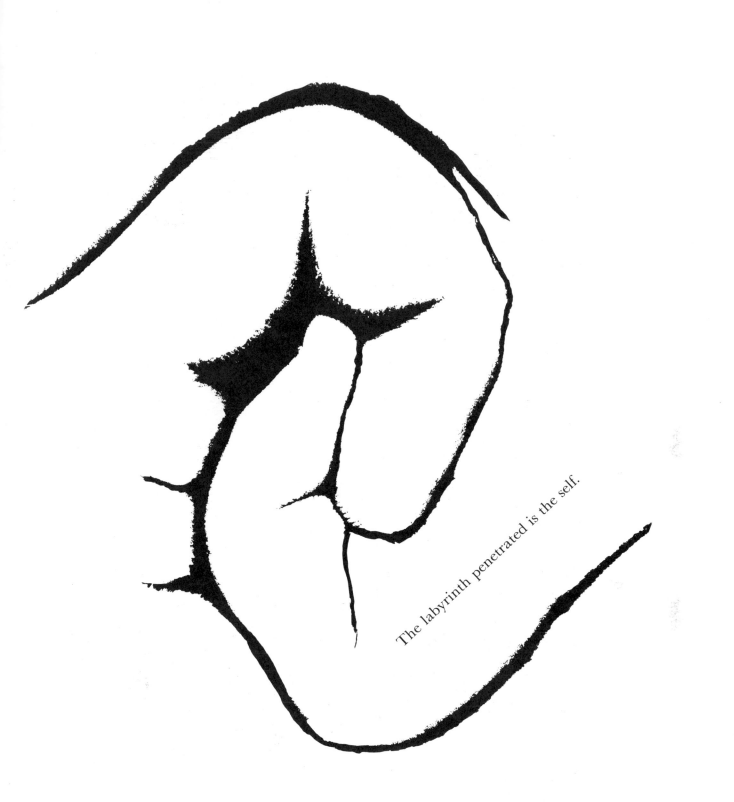

The labyrinth penetrated is the self.

From a mid-thirteenth-century psalter

Setsuji ichimotsu solu fuchū.
The instant you speak about a thing you miss the mark.

—Isshū Miura and Ruth Fuller Sasaki, *The Zen Koan*

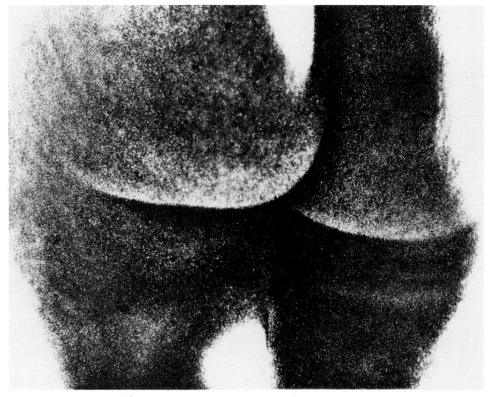

PHOTO BY ROBBIE BERG

Man is the only animal that laughs and weeps;
He is . . . struck with the difference between
what things are and what they ought to be.

—William Hazlitt

In the hereafter each man will be asked to explain why he abstained from those normal pleasures of life to which he was entitled.

—JAMES MICHENER

[95]

THE DIFFERENCE

KNIGHTHAWKS

Let those love now who never loved before.
Let those who always loved now love the more.

—THOMAS PARNELL

BETWEEN...

BY HONORÉ DAUMIER

You see, the upper classes are obsessed with sex, but they contain very little of it themselves. They use up too much sex in their manipulations of power. In effect, they exchange sex for power. So they restrict themselves in their sexuality—whereas the submerged classes have to take their desires for power and plow them back into sex.

—NORMAN MAILER, *The Presidential Papers*

AMERICAN DREAM

Men who are vile flatterers, who have maimed their own fatherlands, each one of them, who have toasted away their liberty first to Philip and now to Alexander, who measure happiness by their lowest desires, and who have overthrown that liberty and that freedom from despotic mastery which to the Greeks of an earlier time were the rules and standards of Good.

—DEMOSTHENES, "On the Crown"

Bread and Circuses sermon

A cultural revolution of mass distraction . . .

Dostoevsky's grand inquisitor was right:

So as not to have to cope with responsible selfhood . . .

of the Miss American Dream contest . . .

Ladies, do you worry about sagging skin?

Here he comes! America's favorite!

Ach, du bist sein leben vertraumen . . .

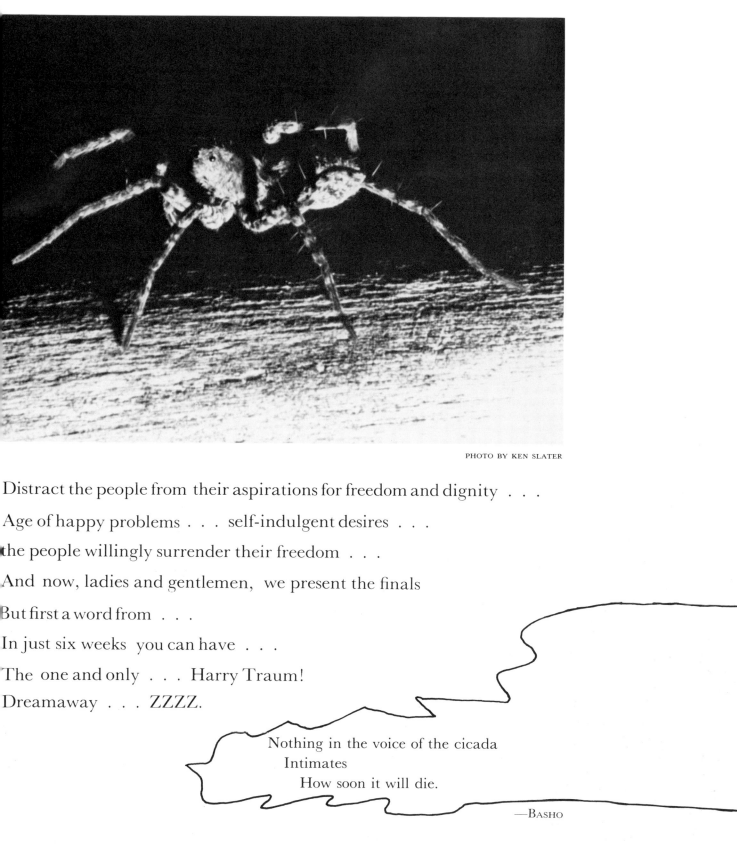

Distract the people from their aspirations for freedom and dignity . . .

Age of happy problems . . . self-indulgent desires . . .

the people willingly surrender their freedom . . .

And now, ladies and gentlemen, we present the finals

But first a word from . . .

In just six weeks you can have . . .

The one and only . . . Harry Traum!

Dreamaway . . . ZZZZ.

Nothing in the voice of the cicada
Intimates
How soon it will die.

—BASHO

[99]

He who ages early does it because he wants to, or better, because he does not want to go on living, because he is incapable of forcing himself to live vigorously. Not well rooted in his own destiny, a parasite on his own life, the flow of time drags him into the past.

—José Ortega y Gasset

"Merry It Is..."

Merry it is while summer lasts
With fowl's song.
But now nears the wind's blast,
And weather strong.
Ai! Ai! but the night is long,
And I with much wrong
Sorrow, and mourn, and fast.

—Old English Song (ca. 1225)

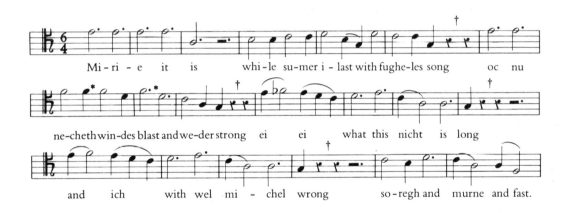

Mi - ri - e it is whi - le su - mer i - last with fughe - les song oc nu

ne - chet win - des blast and we - der strong ei ei what this nicht is long

and ich with wel mi - chel wrong so - regh and murne and fast.

A SIGNPOST
IN SEARCH OF
A DESTINATION

BY RICHARD MOLANDER

Chi gotsugotsu, gotsugotsu chi.
Stupidly steadfast, steadfastly stupid.

—Isshū Miura and Ruth Fuller Sasaki,
The Zen Koan

Do erhieng sich iudas.

BY RICHARD MOLANDER

JAMES GILLRAY (1796)

THE SECOND

Turning and turning in the widening gyre
The falcon cannot hear the falconer;
Things fall apart; the centre cannot hold;
Mere anarchy is loosed upon the world,
The blood-dimmed tide is loosed, and
                                        everywhere
The ceremony of innocence is drowned;
The best lack all conviction, while the
                                        worst
Are full of passionate intensity.
Surely some revelation is at hand;
Surely the Second Coming is at hand.
The Second Coming! Hardly are those words out
When a vast image out of *Spiritus Mundi*
Troubles my sight: somewhere in the sands
                        of the desert

COMING

A shape with lion body and the head of a man,
A gaze blank and pitiless as the sun,
Is moving its slow thighs, while all about it
Reel shadows of the indignant desert birds.
The darkness drops again; but now I know
That twenty centuries of stony sleep
Were vexed to nightmare by a rocking cradle,
And what rough beast, its hour come round
                            at last,
Slouches toward Bethlehem to be born?

—William Butler Yeats (1921)

CHRIST CLIMBED DOWN

Christ climbed down
from His bare Tree
this year
and ran away to where
there were no rootless Christmas trees
hung with candycanes and breakable stars

Christ climbed down
from His bare Tree
this year
and ran away to where
there were no gilded Christmas trees
and no tinsel Christmas trees
and no tinfoil Christmas trees
and no pink plastic Christmas trees
and no gold Christmas trees
and no black Christmas trees
and no powderblue Christmas trees
hung with electric candles
and encircled by tin electric trains
and clever cornball relatives.

Christ climbed down
from His bare Tree
this year
and ran away to where
no intrepid Bible salesmen
covered the territory

in two-tone Cadillacs
and where no Sears Roebuck creches
complete with plastic babe in manger
arrived by parcel post
the babe by special delivery
and where no televised Wise Men
praised the Lord Calvert Whiskey

Christ climbed down
from His bare Tree
this year

IF SOMEONE SHOULD UNMASK

and ran away to where
no fat handshaking stranger
in a red flannel suit
and a fake white beard
went around passing himself off
as some sort of North Pole saint
crossing the desert to Bethlehem
Pennsylvania
in a Volkswagen sled
drawn by rollicking Adirondack reindeer
with German names
and bearing sacks of Humble Gifts
from Saks Fifth Avenue
for everybody's imagined Christ child

Christ climbed down
from His bare Tree
this year
and ran away to where
no Bing Crosby carollers
groaned of a tight Christmas
and where no Radio City angels
iceskated wingless
thru a winter wonderland
into a jinglebell heaven
daily at 8:30
with Midnight Mass matinees

Christ climbed down
from His bare Tree
this year
and softly stole away into
some anonymous Mary's womb again
where in the darknest night
of everybody's anonymous soul
He awaits again
an unimaginable
and impossibly
Immaculate Reconception
the very craziest
of Second Comings

—Lawrence Ferlinghetti

THE ACTORS ...
—Erasmus, *The Praise of Folly*

"The Men's Bath" (1497)   ALBRECHT DÜRER

Why was man created on the last day?
So that he can be told, when pride takes hold of
him: God created the gnat before thee.

—THE TALMUD

Detail from "The Turkish Bath"   DOMINIQUE INGRES

...WHAT ROUGH BEAST
...SLOUCHES TOWARD
BETHLEHEM...?

"Wounded, Fall 1916, Bapaume," from "War" (1924)   OTTO DIX

HELL WE ARE BUILDING HERE
ON EARTH . . .

—NANCY NEWHALL AND ANSEL ADAMS
This Is the American Earth

PHOTO BY RON DOBROWSKI

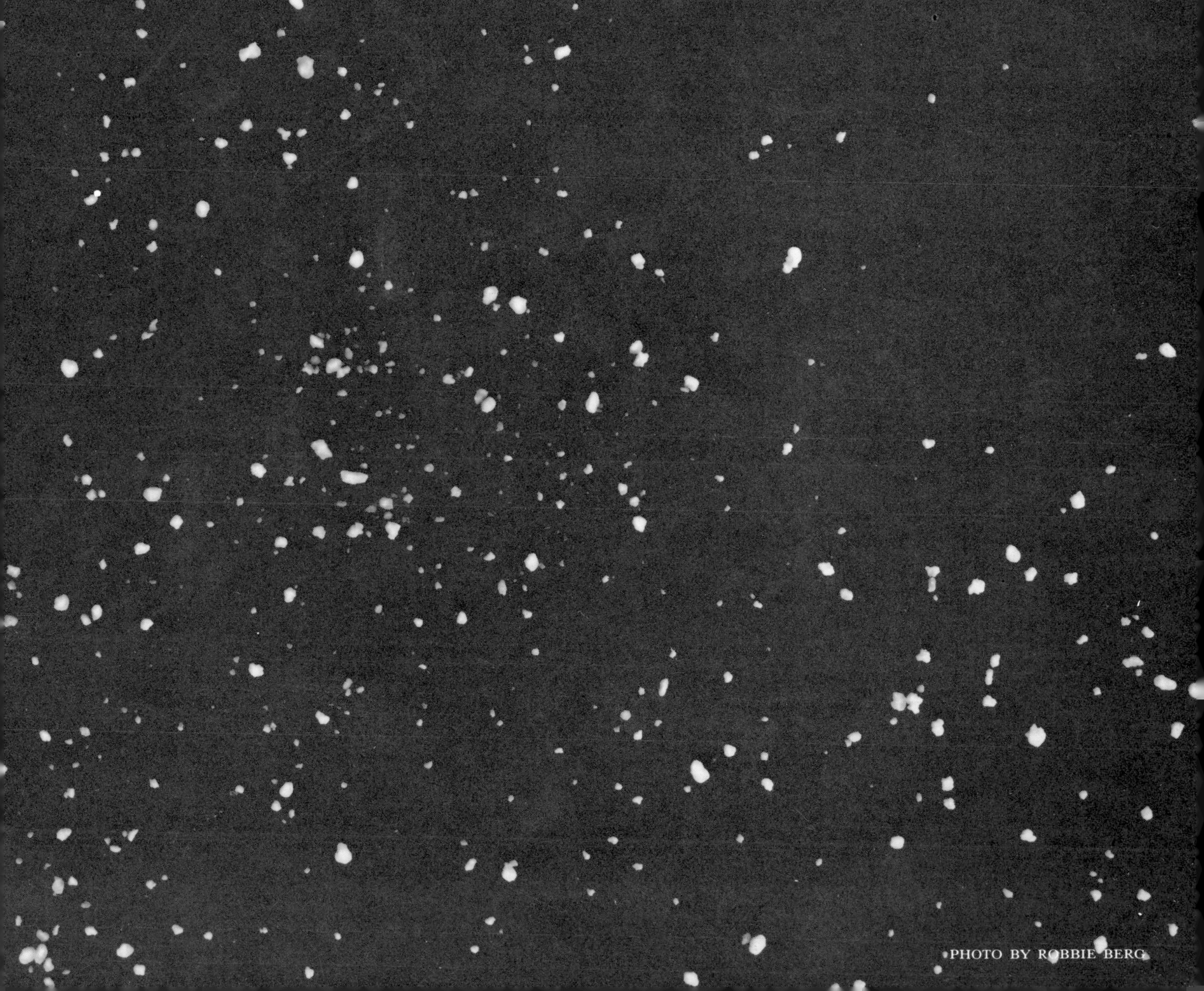

PHOTO BY ROBBIE BERG

IN EVERY GENERATION THERE
HAS TO BE SOME FOOL WHO
WILL SPEAK THE TRUTH AS
HE SEES IT.

—BORIS PASTERNAK

Ah, our ymth, The progenitor of our future. Maybe the earth will be lucky, maybe they will all be sterile.

— Edward Lewis Wallant
The Pawnbroker

PHOTO BY KATHY KRISHNA

The age of our fathers, which was worse than that of our ancestors, produced us, who are about to raise a progeny even more vicious than ourselves.

—HORACE

"Le Ventre Législatif"   Honoré Daumier
(The Legislative Paunch), 1834

ALL MEN ARE EQUAL IN THE
SIGHT OF GOD ...
... BUT SOME ARE MORE
EQUAL THAN OTHERS.

—George Orwell, *Animal Farm*

Concentration
Camps

Protest
Marches

Organized
Religion

From the depths of the far corners of this planet

PHOTO COURTESY OF BARBARA BECKEN

Selective
Service

Political
Conventions

Census
Bureau

Corporations

The Sheep Will Be Slaughtered

It is not I who persecuted the Jews; this was done by the government. I accuse the rulers of abusing my obedience. Obedience has always been praised as a virtue.

—ADOLPH EICHMANN

IT TAKES TIME
TO RUIN A
WORLD...

"La Paix Idylle" (Peace, an Idyll), 1871   HONORÉ DAUMIER

We learn to live with horrors—
evils as old as man, suddenly
expanded into new until they hang
world wide, sky high, above our lives.

Death rides no longer on a pale horse;
Death rides a ray, an atom.

War, winged, rises on strange fires
to leap oceans and continents,
assail the moon, the sun, the stars . . . .

—NANCY NEWHALL AND ANSEL ADAMS
This Is the American Earth

PHOTO BY DAVID RENNIE

. . . BUT TIME IS
ALL IT TAKES

—BERNARD LE BOVIER DE FONTENELLE (1657–1757)

TENDERLY NOW
LET ALL MEN TURN TO THE EARTH

—Nancy Newhall and Ansel Adams
This Is the American Earth

PHOTO BY MIKE LEAF

PHOTO BY MIKE PARENT

SMOKEY THE BEAR SUTRA

Once in the Jurassic, about 150 million years ago, the Great San Buddha in this corner of the Infinite Void gave a great Discourse to all the assembled elements and energies: to the standing beings, the walking beings, the flying beings, and the sitting beings—even grasses, to the number of thirteen billion, each one born from a seed, were assembled there: a Discourse concerning Enlightenment on the planet Earth.

"In some future time, there will be a continent called America. It will have great centers of power called such as Pyramid Lake, Walden Pond, Mt. Rainier, Big Sur, Everglades, and so forth; and powerful nerves and channels such as Columbia River, Mississippi River, and Grand Canyon. The human race in that era will get into troubles all over its head, and practically wreck everything in spite of its own strong intelligent Buddha-nature."

"The twisting strata of the great mountains and the pulsings of great volcanoes are my love burning deep in the earth. My obstinate compassion is schist and basalt and granite, to be mountains, to bring down the rain. In that future American Era I shall enter a new form: to cure the world of loveless knowledge that seeks with blind hunger; and mindless rage eating food that will not fill it."

And he showed himself in his true form of

SMOKEY THE BEAR.

A handsome smokey-colored brown bear standing on his hind legs, showing that he is aroused and watchful.

Bearing in his right paw the Shovel that digs to the truth beneath appearances; cuts the roots of useless attachments, and flings damp sand on the fires of greed and war;

His left paw in the Mudra of Comradely Display—indicating that all creatures have the full right to live to their limits and that deer, rabbits, chipmunks, snakes, dandelions, and lizards all grow in the realm of the Dharma;

Wearing the blue work overalls symbolic of slaves and laborers, the countless men oppressed by a civilization that claims to save but only destroys;

Wearing the broad-brimmed hat of the West, symbolic of the forces that guard the Wilderness, which is the Natural State of the Dharma and the True Path of man on earth; all true paths lead through mountains—
With a halo of smoke and flame behind, the forest fires of the kali-yuga, fires caused by the stupidity of those who think things can be gained and lost whereas in truth all is contained vast and free in the Blue Sky and Green Earth of One Mind;

Round-bellied to show his kind nature and that the great earth has food enough for everyone who loves her and trusts her;

Trampling underfoot wasteful freeways and needless suburbs; smashing the worms of capitalism and totalitarianism;

Indicating the Task: his followers, becoming free of cars, houses, canned food, universities, and shoes, master the Three Mysteries of their own Body, Speech, and Mind, and fearlessly chop down the rotten trees and prune out the sick limbs of this country America and then burn the leftover trash.

Wrathful but Calm, Austere but Comic, Smokey the Bear will Illuminate those who would help him; but for those who would hinder or slander him,

HE WILL PUT THEM OUT.

Thus his great Mantra:

Namah samanta vajranam chanda maharoshana
Sphataya hum traka ham mam

"I DEDICATE MYSELF TO THE UNIVERSAL DIAMOND
BE THIS RAGING FURY DESTROYED"

And he will protect those who love woods and rivers, Gods and animals, hobos and madmen, prisoners and sick people, musicians, playful women, and hopeful children;

And if anyone is threatened by advertising, air pollution, or the police, they should chant SMOKEY THE BEAR'S WAR SPELL:

DROWN THEIR BUTTS
CRUSH THEIR BUTTS
DROWN THEIR BUTTS
CRUSH THEIR BUTTS

And SMOKEY THE BEAR will surely appear to put the enemy out with his vajra-shovel.

Now those who recite this Sutra and then try to put it in practice will accumulate merit as countless as the sands of Arizona and Nevada,
Will help save the planet Earth from total oil slick,

Will enter the age of harmony of man and nature,
Will win the tender love and caresses of men, women, and beasts
Will always have ripe blackberries to eat and a sunny spot under a pine tree to sit at,

AND IN THE END WILL WIN HIGHEST PERFECT ENLIGHTENMENT,

thus have we heard.

(may be reproduced free forever)

—ANONYMOUS (well-known American poet)

Bluebells—
Cockleshells—
EEvie, Ivy, Overheads!

JUMP

I like coffee—
I like tea—
I want Jane—
To jump with me!

HOP SCOTCH
HOP SCOTCH

TELL
THE
TEACHER

WHO'S
THE
BOSS

HOP
SCOTCH
HOP
SCOTCH

BY SAGE SIGERSON

One-Two-Three-A-Larry—
My first name is Mary—
Don't you think that I look cute—
In my mother's bathing suit?

JUMP   JUMP

[125]

The Children's Charter

President Hoover's White House Conference on Child Health and Protection, recognizing the rights of the child as the first rights of citizenship, pledges itself to these aims for the children of America

I For every child spiritual and moral training to help him to stand firm under the pressure of life

II For every child understanding and the guarding of his personality as his most precious right

III For every child a home and that love and security which a home provides; and for that child who must receive foster care, the nearest substitute for his own home

IV For every child full preparation for his birth, his mother receiving prenatal, natal, and postnatal care; and the establishment of such protective measures as will make child-bearing safer

V For every child health protection from birth through adolescence, including: periodical health examinations and, where needed, care of specialists and hospital treatment; regular dental examination and care of the teeth; protective and preventive measures against communicable diseases; the insuring of pure food, pure milk, and pure water

VI For every child from birth through adolescence, promotion of health, including health instruction and a health program, wholesome physical and mental recreation, with teachers and leaders adequately trained

VII For every child a dwelling place safe, sanitary, and wholesome, with reasonable provisions for privacy, free from conditions which tend to thwart his development; and a home environment harmonious and enriching

VIII For every child a school which is safe from hazards, sanitary, properly equipped, lighted, and ventilated. For younger children nursery schools and kindergartens to supplement home care

IX For every child a community which recognizes and plans for his needs, protects him against physical dangers, moral hazards, and disease; provides him with safe and wholesome places for play and recreation; and makes provision for his cultural and social needs

X For every child an education which, through the discovery and development of his individual abilities, prepares him for life; and through training and vocational guidance prepares him for a living which will yield him the maximum of satisfaction

XI For every child such teaching and training as will prepare him for successful parenthood, homemaking, and the rights of citizenship; and, for parents, supplementary training to fit them to deal wisely with the problems of parenthood

XII For every child education for safety and protection against accidents to which modern conditions subject him—those to which he is directly exposed and those which, through loss or maiming of his parents, affect him indirectly

XIII For every child who is blind, deaf, crippled, or otherwise physically handicapped, and for the child who is mentally handicapped, such measures as will early discover and diagnose his handicap, provide care and treatment, and so train him that he may become an asset to society rather than a liability. Expenses of these services should be borne publicly where they cannot be privately met

XIV For every child who is in conflict with society the right to be dealt with intelligently as society's charge, not society's outcast; with the home, the school, the church, the court and the institution when needed, shaped to return him whenever possible to the normal stream of life

XV For every child the right to grow up in a family with an adequate standard of living and the security of a stable income as the surest safeguard against social handicaps

XVI For every child protection against labor that stunts growth, either physical or mental, that limits education, that deprives children of the right of comradeship, of play, and of joy

XVII For every rural child as satisfactory schooling and health services as for the city child, and an extension to rural families of social, recreational, and cultural facilities

XVIII To supplement the home and the school in the training of youth, and to return to them those interests of which modern life tends to cheat children, every stimulation and encouragement should be given to the extension and development of the voluntary youth organizations

XIX To make everywhere available these minimum protections of the health and welfare of children, there should be a district, county, or community organization for health, education, and welfare, with full-time officials, coordinating with a state-wide program which will be responsive to a nation-wide service of general information, statistics, and scientific research. This should include:

(a) Trained, full-time public health officials, with public health nurses, sanitary inspection, and laboratory workers

(b) Available hospital beds

(c) Full-time public welfare service for the relief, aid, and guidance of children in special need due to poverty, misfortune, or behavior difficulties, and for the protection of children from abuse, neglect, exploitation, or moral hazard

For EVERY child these rights, regardless of race, or color, or situation, wherever he may live under the protection of the American flag

PHOTO (1917) COURTESY OF BARBARA BECKEN

I
FIGURED
OUT . . .

that in a
way we
never die
at all . . .

if people
have children
and children
have children—

in a way
we go on
living

just like
the branches
of a tree

—Theodore Isaac Rubin,
Lisa and David

Esto es peor.

"Esto Es Peor" (This Is Worse)　　　Francisco de Goya y Lucientes

*'Tis sweet to feel
by what fine-spun
threads our
affections are drawn
together.*
    —Lawrence Sterne

THE BIRTH OF CHILDREN
IS THE DEATH OF PARENTS

—Georg Wilhelm Friedrich Hegel

PHOTO BY CARL COFFMAN

The most incomprehensible thing about the world is that it is comprehensible.

[130]

Group Picture (1868)

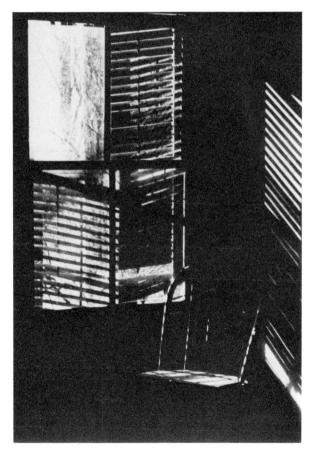

WONDERS ARE MANY,
AND NONE IS MORE
WONDERFUL THAN MAN.

—SOPHOCLES

MATRIMONIAL-HARMONICS.

JAMES GILLRAY (1805)

Feed on us before you bury us.

—Anaïs Nin, *The Diary of Anaïs Nin*, Vol. III

"Self Portrait"   DAVE RENNIE

We all like to be loved or hated; it is a sign that we shall be remembered, that we did not "not exist." For this reason many unable to create love have created hate. That too is remembered.

—JOHN FOWLES, *The Aristos*

William Cody ("Buffalo Bill"), Denver, 1898

Loneliness is being all by yourself, even when there are people around.

—James A. Smith

The young have aspirations that never come to pass, the old reminiscences of what never happened.

—Saki

WHAT WE CANNOT SPEAK ABOUT, WE MUST CONSIGN TO SILENCE.

—Ludwig Wittgenstein, *Tractatus Logico-Philosophicus*

PHOTO BY CARL COFFMAN

CITY...

. . . Millions of People Who Do Not Even Need to Know Each Other . . .

—ARTHUR RIMBAUD

. . . trying to work myself up . . . it's a measley manner of existence . . . to suffer fifty weeks of the year for the sake of a two-week vacation. . . . And always to have to get ahead of the next fella . . . —that's how to build a future.

—Biff, *Death of a Salesman* BY ARTHUR MILLER

Love consists in this:
    that two solitudes protect and touch
and greet each other.

—Rainer Maria Rilke

You can't eat the orange and throw the peel away—A man is not a piece of fruit! . . .

—ARTHUR MILLER, *Death of a Salesman*

The sight of human affairs deserves admiration and pity. And he is not insensible who pays them the undemonstrative tribute of a sigh which is not a sob, and of a smile that is not a grin.

—JOSEPH CONRAD

" 'Treat this dinner as you would the enemy.' "

From *Chatterbox* (1904)

1658 Receipt: Fricassee of Chickens

Kill your chickens, pull skin and feathers off together, cut them in thin slices, season them with thime and lemmon minced, nutmeg and salt, and handful of sorrel minced, and then fry it well with six spoonsfuls of water, and some fresh butter; when it is tender, take three spoonsfuls of verjuice, one spoonful of sugar, beat it together, to dish it with sippets about.

[142]

Recipe for Preserved Children

Take 1 large field, half a dozen children, 2 or 3 small dogs, a pinch of brook and some pebbles. Mix the children and dogs well together; put them on the field, stirring constantly. Pour the brook over the pebbles, sprinkle the field with flowers, spread over all a deep blue sky and bake in the sun. When brown, set away to cool in a bath tub.

—A Cook's Tour of Kauai, quoted in Don Fabun,
The Dynamics of Change

BY JOHN T. MC CUTCHEON (1904)

LET'S

My blood was on fire, and blossomed forth as my soul cried aloud and sang. I was a boy of fifteen or sixteen with my head full of Latin and Greek and poetry. I was all ardor and ambition and my fancy was laden with the artist's dreams.

—Hermann Hesse, *Steppenwolf*

LIVE

I remember my youth and the feeling that will never come back any more, the feeling that I could last forever, outlast the sea, the earth and all men.

—JOSEPH CONRAD

These were the woods the river and sea
  Where a boy
 In the listening
Summertime of the dead whispered the truth of his joy
To the trees and the stones and the fish in the tide.
  And the mystery
  Sang alive
Still in the water and the singingbirds.

—DYLAN THOMAS

START
AGAIN . . .

En ma fin est mon commencement.

> —Inscription embroidered
> upon the chair of
> state of Mary Stuart,
> Queen of Scots

The beginning and the end are common.

> —HERACLITUS OF EPHESUS

[146]

Life in the twentieth century is like a parachute jump: you have to get it right the first time.

—MARGARET MEAD

[147]

Whoever despises himself still esteems the despiser within himself.

—FRIEDRICH NIETZSCHE
Beyond Good and Evil

'71
Happy Birthday, from Jeff

by Jeff Danforth

The night surrounds me, a photograph unglued from its frame. The lining of a coat ripped open like two shells of an oyster. The day and night unglued, and I falling in between, not knowing on which layer I was resting, whether it was the cold grey upper leaf of dawn, or the dark layer of night.

—ANAÏS NIN, *The House of Incest*

He whom the gods favor dies in youth.

—Plautus

by Bobby Stifft

Arms and the Boy

Let the boy try along this bayonet blade
How cold steel is, and keen with hunger of blood;
Blue with all malice, like a madman's flash;
And thinly drawn with famishing for flesh.

Lend him to stroke these blind, blunt bullet-heads
Which long to nuzzle in the hearts of lads,
Or give him cartridges of fine zinc teeth,
Sharp with the sharpness of grief and death.

For his teeth seem for laughing round an apple.
There lurk no claws behind his fingers supple;
And God will grow no talons at his heels,
Nor antlers through the thickness of his curls.

—Wilfred Owen

The dreaming child
is on a threshold
between life and death
    Neither are monsters
    Neither are friends

—C. L. WHITE

PHOTO BY RON POGUE

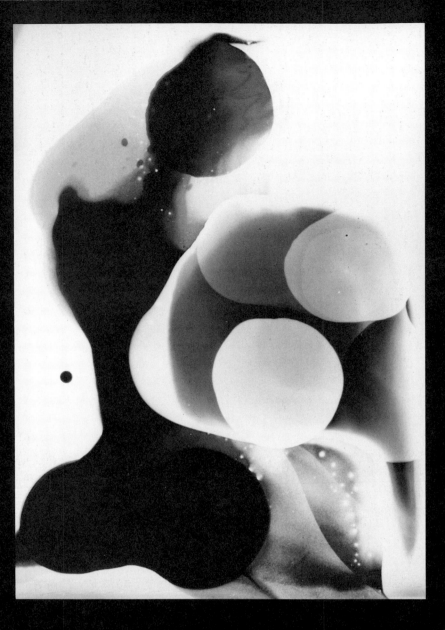

Scene one

Lips   summon up
        the moist
Rises up Osiris
Cut flesh in the fields
        She is the Mother
            the passion
                the sea
                    slept
                    slithering
Serpent   of two tongues
Tomorrow I will leave her and need her
                before the next dawn

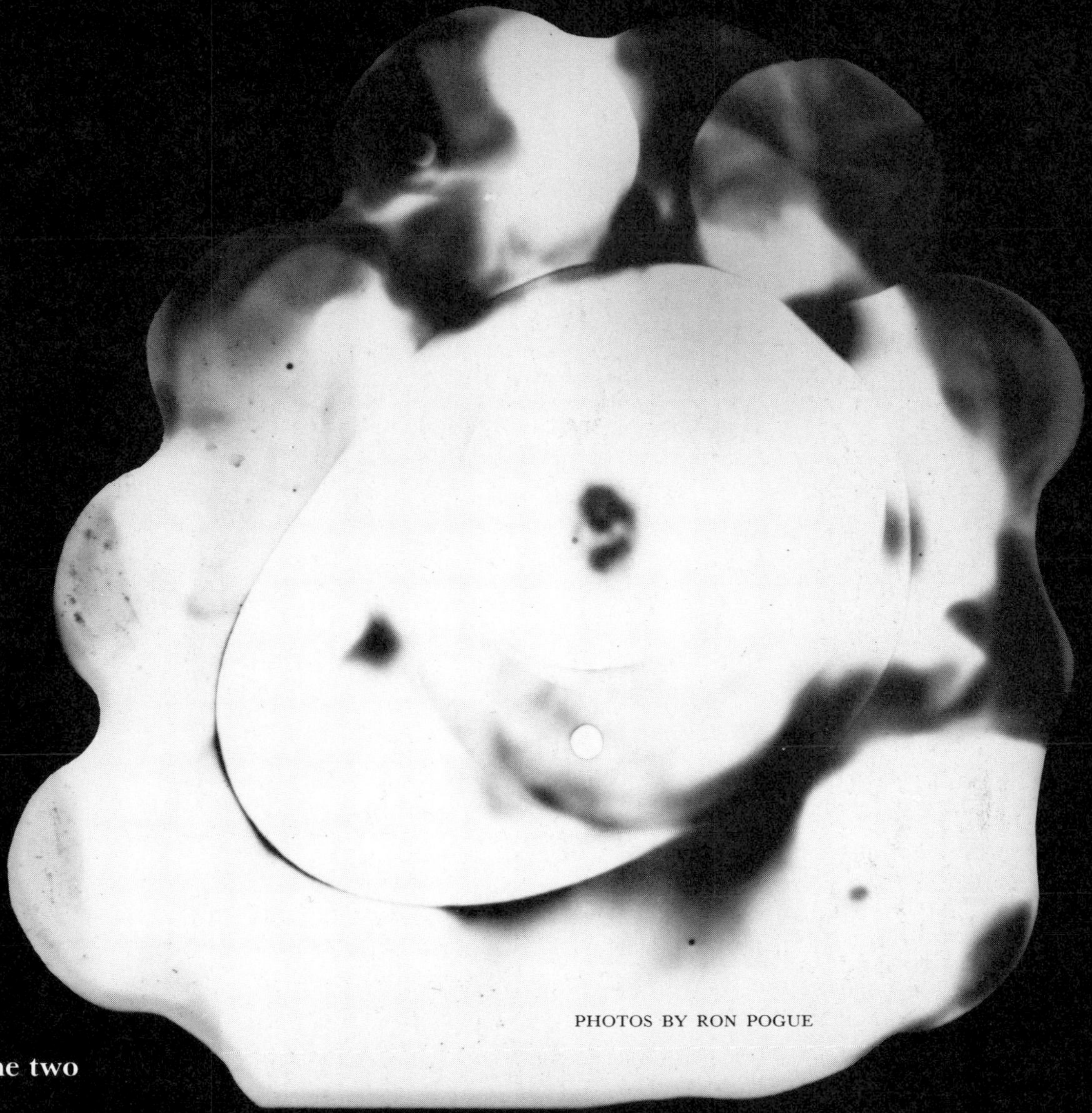

PHOTOS BY RON POGUE

Scene two

Inside the canal
seed-pod prowling
in the warm
on its way
in her   a new life
Your home   call it
Paradise
it might not end
ecstasy   beginnings
Downdriftout   shattering
the end   cut the cord
on the way to
Extinction
a hulk of quivering flesh

Scene three

He comes out
slime covered
Not knowing his past
dark   eternal   sleep
Life spent
trying to create
the creation

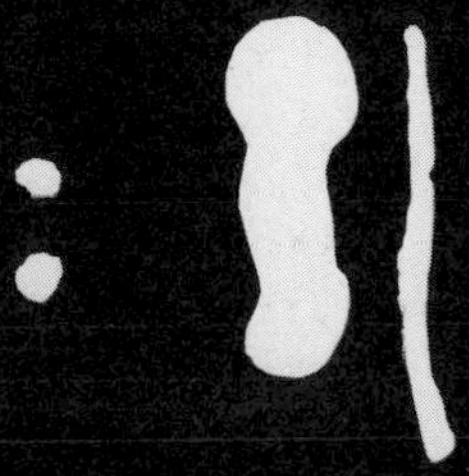

—WILL MAKYNEN

BY DENNIS DE WEESE

This cave is grave; this womb is tomb. We are not yet born; we are dead. The souls of children not yet born are the souls of ancestors dead. The underlying idea is reincarnation. . . . The wanderings of the soul after death are prenatal adventures; a journey by water, in a ship which is itself a Goddess, to the gates of rebirth.

—NORMAN O. BROWN, *Love's Body*

THE PRAISE
OF FOLLY

DILETTANTI-THEATRICALS; — or — a Peep at the Green Room — Vide Pic Nic Orgies.

JAMES GILLRAY (1803)

The full warm feeling in my heart for living nature which flooded me with so much joy, which transformed the world about me into a paradise, is now becoming a source of unbearable torment for me, a torturing demon which pursues me everywhere.

—JOHANN WOLFGANG VON GOETHE

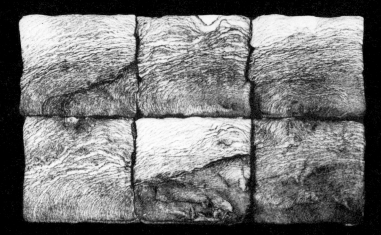

"The San Andreas Fault"   RICHARD MOLANDER

A mass of hands reaching for me.
Grabbing at me—trying to snuff
out my life
Squeezing, choking.

—SANDY DECKER, *The Empty Spoon*

My entire soul is a cry, and all my
work the commentary on that cry.

—NIKOS KAZANTZAKIS

"The Prisoners"   KAETHE KOLLWITZ

DEATH IS A REFLECTION
OF LIFE

PHOTO BY BOB STORY

I knew that all the hundred thousand pieces of life's game were in my pocket. A glimpse of its meaning had stirred my reason and I was determined to begin afresh. I would sample its tortures once more and shudder again at its senselessness. I would traverse not once more, but often, the hell of my inner being. One day I would be a better hand at the game.

One day I would learn how to laugh.

—HERMANN HESSE, *Steppenwolf*

. . . LEARN HOW
TO LAUGH

BY ALBRECHT DÜRER

NIGHTMARE NUMBER THREE

We had expected everything but revolt
And I kind of wonder myself when they started thinking—
But there's no dice in that now.
                              I've heard fellows say
They must have planned it for years and maybe they did.
Looking back, you can find little incidents here and there,
Like the concrete-mixer in Jersey eating the wop
Or the roto press that printed "Fiddle-dee-dee!"
In a three-color process all over Senator Sloop,
Just as he was making a speech. The thing about that
Was, how could it walk upstairs? But it *was* upstairs,
Clicking and mumbling in the Senate Chamber,
They had to knock out the wall to take it away
And the wrecking crew said it grinned.
                              It was only the best
Machines, of course, the super human machines,
The ones we'd built to be better than flesh and bone,
But the cars were in it, of course . . .
                              And they haunted us
Like rabbits through the cramped streets on that Bloody Monday,
The Madison Avenue busses leading the charge.
The busses were pretty bad—but I'll not forget
The smash of glass when the Dusenberg left the show-room
And pinned three brokers to the Racquet Club steps,
Or the long howl of the horns when they saw the men run,
When they saw them looking for holes in the solid ground . . .

I guess they were tired of being ridden in,
And stopped and started by pygmies for silly ends,
Of wrapping cheap cigarettes and bad chocolate bars,
Collecting nickels and waving platinum hair,
And letting six million people live in a town.
I guess it was that. I guess they got tired of us
And the whole smell of human hands.
                              But it was a shock

BORDER BY SAGE SIGERSON

To climb sixteen flights of stairs to Art Zuckow's office
(Nobody took the elevators twice)
And find him strangled to death in a nest of telephones,
The octopus-tendrils waving over his head,
And a sort of quiet humming filling the air . . .
Do they eat? . . . There was red . . . But I did not stop to look.
And it's lonely here on the roof.

                      For a while I thought
That window-cleaner would make it, and keep me company.
But they got him with his own hoist at the sixteenth floor
And dragged him in with a squeal.
You see, they cooperate. Well, we taught them that,
And it's fair enough, I suppose. You see, we built them.
We taught them to think for themselves.
It was bound to come. You can see it was bound to come.
And it won't be so bad, in the country. I hate to think
Of the reapers, running wild in the Kansas fields,
And the transport planes like hawks on a chickenyard,
But the horses might help. We might make a deal with the horses.
At least you've more chance, out there.

                          And they need us too.
They're bound to realize that when they calm down.
They'll need oil and spare parts and adjustments and tuning up.
Slaves? Well, in a way, you know, we were slaves before.
There won't be so much real difference—honest there won't.
(I wish I hadn't looked into that beauty-parlor
And seen what was happening there.
But those are female machines and a bit high-strung.)
Oh, we'll settle down. We'll arrange it. We'll compromise.
It wouldn't make sense to wipe out the whole human race.
Why, I bet if I went to my old Plymouth now
(Of course, you'd have to do it in a tactful way)
And said, "Look here! Who got you the swell French horn?"
He wouldn't turn me over to the police cars.
At least I don't *think* he would.

                    Oh, it's going to be jake.
There won't be so much real difference—honest, there won't—
And I'd go down in a minute and take my chance—
I'm a good American and I always liked them—
Except for one small detail that bothers me
And that's the food proposition. Because you see,
The concrete mixer may have made a mistake,
And it looks like just high spirits.
But, if it's got so they like the flavor . . . well . . .

            —STEPHEN VINCENT BENÉT

A DESTINATION

BY LANET STROBEL

People used to buy things because they needed the things to survive, not because the things needed the people to survive.

—MASON WILLIAMS, *The FCC Rapport*

IN SEARCH OF
A SIGN

Suburbia lives imaginatively in Bonanza-land.

—MARSHALL MCLUHAN AND QUENTIN FIORE
The Medium Is the Massage

HAVING FUN WISH YOU

YOUR
SYMBOL
HAS JUST
LOST ITS
STATUS

BY BOBBY STIFFT

WE'RE HERE LOVE
Bobby

[169]

WE HAVE NO ALTERNATIVE BUT PATTERN RECOGNITION X FACED WITH AN INFORMATION OVERLOAD WE HAVE NO ALTERNATIVE BUT PATTERN RECOGNITION X FACED WITH AN INFORMATION OVERLOAD WE HAVE NO ALTERNATIVE BUT PATTERN RECOGNITION X FACED WITH AN INFORMATION OVERLOAD WE HAVE NO ALTERNATIVE BUT PATTERN RECOGNITION X FACED WITH AN INFORMATION OVERLOAD WE HAVE NO ALTERNATIVE BUT PATTERN RECOGNITION X FACED WITH AN INFORMATION OVERLOAD WE HAVE NO ALTERNATIVE BUT PATTERN RECOGNITION X FACED WITH AN INFORMATION OVERLOAD WE HAVE NO ALTERNATIVE BUT PATTERN RECOGNITION X FACED WITH AN INFORMATION OVERLOAD WE HAVE NO ALTERNATIVE BUT PATTERN RECOGNITION X FACED WITH AN INFORMATION OVERLOAD

PROGRAM BY Bruce Scoles

TRUTH HAS NO WORDS.
WORDS CAN ONLY CIR-
CUMSCRIBE THAT WHICH
CANNOT BE SAID . . .

PHOTO BY RON POGUE

BY C. L. WHITE

[173]

SINBAD THE SAILOR
AND TINBAD THE TAILOR

and Jinbad the Jailer and Whinbad the Whaler
and Ninbad the Nailer and Finbad the Failer
and Binbad the Bailer and Pinbad the Pailer
and Minbad the Mailer and Hinbad the Hailer
and Rinbad the Railer and Dinbad the Kailer
and Vinbad the Quailer and Linbad the Yailer
and Xinbad the Phthailer.

—JAMES JOYCE, *Ulysses*

WHINBAD

NINBAD THE NAILER

BINBAD THE BAILER

MINBAD THE MAILER
RINBAD THE RAILER

HE WHO WONDERS DISCOVERS
THAT THIS IS IN ITSELF
A WONDER.

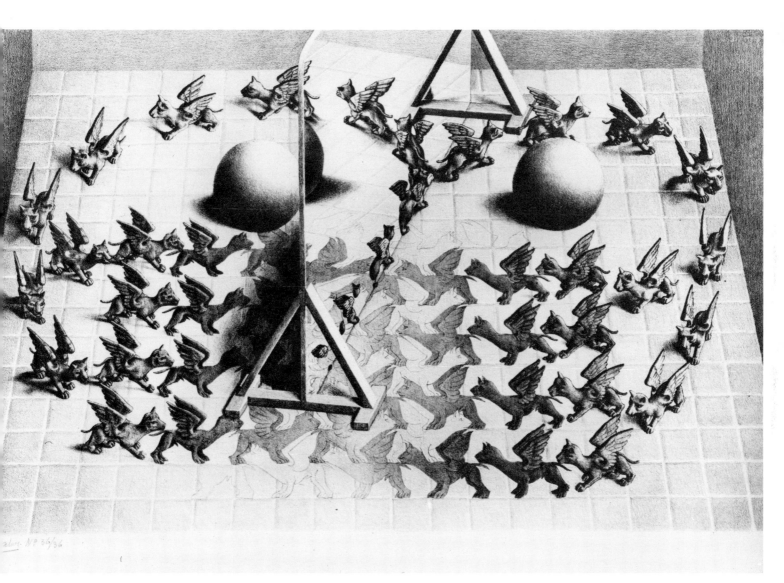

"Magic Mirror"   M. C. ESCHER

VINBAD THE QUAILER
        XINBAD THE PHTHAILER

TRAJAN WAS A FISHER OF FROGS

BY W. HEATH ROBINSON

The secret waits for the insight
of eyes unclouded by longing;
those who are bound by desire
see only the outward container.

—LAO TZU, *The Way of Life*

BORDER BY SAGE SIGERSON

BEWARE: DO NOT READ THIS POEM

tonite   . "Thriller" was
abt an ol woman   , so vain she
surrounded herself w/
           many mirrors

it got so bad that finally she
locked herself indoors & her
whole life became the
           mirrors

one day the villagers broke
into her house   ,   but she was too
swift for them   .   she disappeared
           into a mirror

each tenant who bought the house
after that   ,   lost a loved one to
           the ol woman in the mirror   :
           first a little girl
           then a young woman
           then the young woman/s husband

the hunger of this poem is legendary
it has taken in many victims
back off from this poem
it has drawn in yr feet
back off from this poem
it has drawn in yr legs

back off from this poem
it is a greedy mirror
you are into this poem   from
      the waist down
nobody can hear you can they   ?
this poem has had you up to here
      belch

this poem aint got no manners
you cant call out frm this poem
relax now & go w/ this poem
move & roll on to this poem
do not resist this poem
this poem has yr eyes
this poem has his head
this poem has his arms
this poem has his fingers
this poem has his fingertips

this poem is the reader & the
reader this poem

statistic   : the us bureau of missing persons reports
              that in 1968 over 100,000 people disappeared
              leaving no solid clues
                    nor trace   only
              a space   in the lives of their friends

—Ishmael Reed

'Tis the intent and business of the stage
to copy out the follies of the age,
to hold to every man a faithful glass,
and show him of what species he's an ass

—Sir John Vanbrugh
The Provoked Wife (1697)

James Gillray (1802)

CREDO
QUIA

by Albrecht Dürer

ABSURDUM EST

THE SECRET
WAITS

Moreover, it is very hard for a speaker to be appropriate when many of
his hearers will scarce believe that he is truthful.

—PERICLES, *Funeral Oration*

I am enmeshed in my lies, and I want absolution. I cannot tell the truth because I have felt the heads of men in my womb. The truth would be death-dealing and I prefer fairytales. I am wrapped in lies which do not penetrate my soul. As if the lies I tell were like costumes. The shell of mystery can break and grow again over night. But the moment I step into the cavern of my lies I drop into darkness. I see a face which stares at me like the glance of a cross-eyed man.

—Anaïs Nin
The House of Incest

The heart of man and the bottom
of the sea are unfathomable.

—Jewish proverb

[183]

Everyman (ca. 1500 A.D.)

Dramatis Personae

Messenger

God

Death

Everyman

Fellowship

Cousin

Kindred

Goods

Doctor

Good Deeds

Knowledge

Confession

Beauty

Strength

Discretion

Five Wits

Angel

Here beginneth a treatise how the High Father of Heaven sendeth Death to summon every creature to come and give account of their lives in this world, and is in the manner of a play.

(Enter MESSENGER, as Prologue)

MESSENGER:

   I pray you all give your audience,
And here this matter with reverence,
By figure a moral play.
The *Summoning of Everyman* called it is,
That of our lives and ending shows
How transitory we be all day.
This matter is wondrous precious,
But the intent of it is more gracious,
And sweet to bear away.
The story saith: Man, in the beginning
Look well, and take good heed to the ending,
Be you never so gay!
Ye think sin in the beginning full sweet,
Which in the end causeth the soul to weep,
When the body lieth in clay. . . .

PHOTO BY ROBBIE BERG

Men are never convinced of your reasons, of your sincerity, of the seriousness of your suffering except by your death. So long as you are alive, your case is doubtful; you have a right only to their skepticism.

—ALBERT CAMUS, *The Fall*

UNMASK THE ACTORS...

In short, you see, the essential is to cease being free and to obey, in repentance, a greater rogue than oneself. When we are all guilty, that will be democracy.

—ALBERT CAMUS, *The Fall*

Here a question arises: whether it is better to be loved than feared, or the reverse. The answer is, of course, that it would be best to be both loved and feared. But since the two rarely come together, anyone compelled to choose will find greater security in being feared than in being loved. . . . Men are less concerned about offending someone they have cause to love than someone they have cause to fear.

—NICCOLÒ MACHIAVELLI, *The Prince*

BY PHIL LINK

The great twentieth-century
equation is that I = you.

And the great twentieth-century
envy is that I am less than you.

—JOHN FOWLES, *The Aristos*

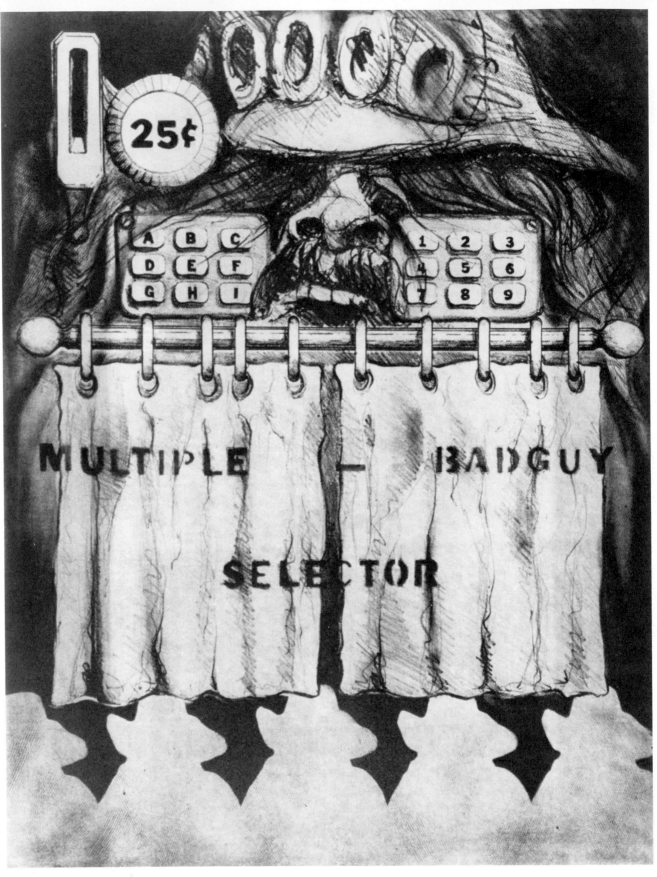

"81 Bad Guys"   John Pollock

If we want our lives to bear fruit, we must make the decision which harmonizes with the fearsome rhythm of our times.

—Nikos Kazantzakis

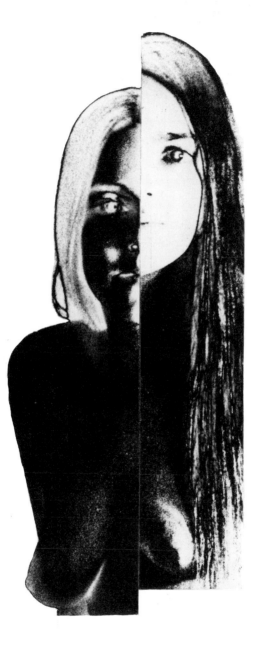

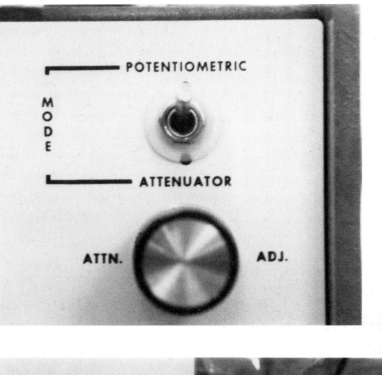

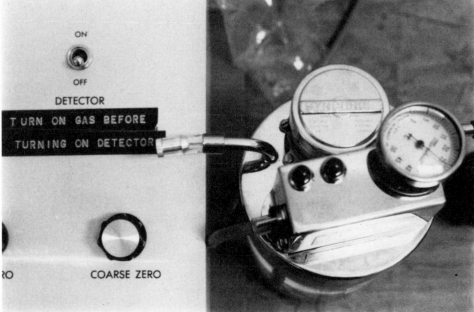

PHOTOS BY JACK FOLSOM

[189]

We fear to become victims of dehumanization by industrialization and mechanization, but that is not where the danger lies. The danger lies in everyone's *private dehumanization*, which becomes contagious, universal, and can end in crime.

—ANAÏS NIN, *Novel of the Future*

PHOTO BY PAUL JESSWEIN

effects of a 5-MT blast

People close to the detonation, within 3 miles of ground zero, are not likely to survive the blast and thermal effects. Out from the total destruction ring, chances for survival improve markedly. The percentage of the population surviving blast and thermal effects increases rapidly as the distance from ground zero increases, but a large portion of the survivors would be exposed to the lethal effects of radioactive fallout.

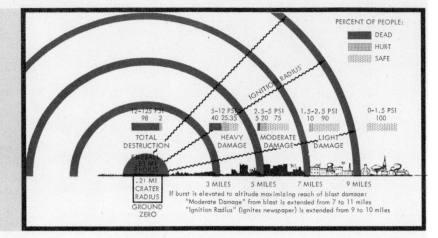

effects of a 20-MT blast

While this amounts to a fourfold increase in megatonnage over the five-megaton weapon the same blast and thermal effects occur at less than twice the distance from ground zero. As in the case of the five-megaton weapon, millions of people could survive these initial effects.

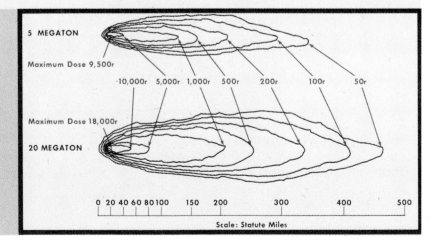

unshielded maximum equivalent radiation dose contours

Geographical coverage of radioactive fallout from 5 to 20 megaton surface blasts would be extensive. Based on a 25 mph upper air wind, significant amounts of fallout from these weapons would be deposited over thousands of square miles of area downwind.

A dose of over 200 roentgens could cause disabling illness and some deaths. At 450 roentgens there is a 50-50 probability of death, and over 600 roentgens would leave few survivors.

In an actual attack, fallout from several weapons could overlap increasing radiation levels further.

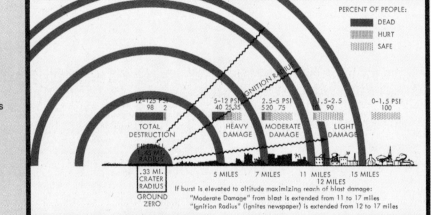

From Office of Civil Defense Pamphlet TR-39, December 1967

Outside Semimounded Plywood Box Shelter

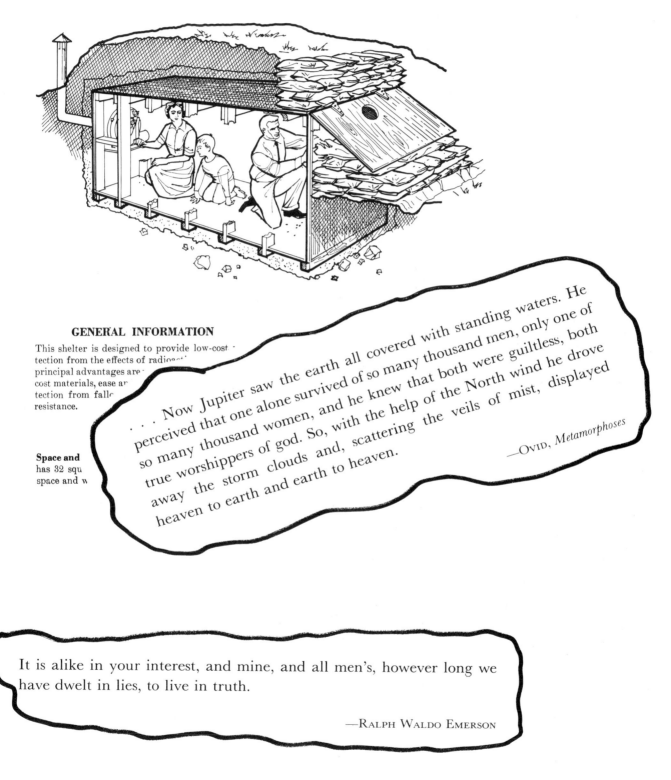

GENERAL INFORMATION

This shelter is designed to provide low-cost ⋯
tection from the effects of radio⋯
principal advantages are ⋯
cost materials, ease a⋯
tection from fall⋯
resistance.

Space and
has 32 squ⋯
space and ⋯

. . . Now Jupiter saw the earth all covered with standing waters. He perceived that one alone survived of so many thousand men, only one of so many thousand women, and he knew that both were guiltless, both true worshippers of god. So, with the help of the North wind he drove away the storm clouds and, scattering the veils of mist, displayed heaven to earth and earth to heaven.

—Ovid, *Metamorphoses*

It is alike in your interest, and mine, and all men's, however long we have dwelt in lies, to live in truth.

—Ralph Waldo Emerson

WE SHOULD DO
A LOT OF THINGS

Courtesy, Museum of Fine Arts, Boston; Maria Antoinette Evans Fund

Bronze Mongolian boy looking at two jade birds

[194]

It is the business of the future to be dangerous.

—ALFRED NORTH WHITEHEAD

The PIC-NIC. ORCHESTRA.

JAMES GILLRAY (1802)

. . . have I not reason to hate and despise myself? Indeed I do, and chiefly for not having hated and despised the world enough.

—WILLIAM HAZLITT, "On the Pleasures of Hating"

"Oh . . . you should do a lot of things,
but there's nothing to do."

—Linda, *Death of a Salesman*
BY ARTHUR MILLER

'I SHALL NEVER SPEAK AGAIN.'

A DROLL story is narrated of a dog to which the power of speech was seemingly given by the art of a ventriloquist. The dog and his master one day arrived at a country inn, the latter with only a shilling in his pocket. He went in and sat down at a table and prepared to order a meal.

'Well, what will you have?' asked the landlord.

The ventriloquist gave his order, and then, turning to the dog, he asked, 'What will you have?'

'I'll take a ham sandwich,' was the dog's immediate reply.

The inn-keeper was breathless for a moment with astonishment.

'What did you say?' he asked.

'I said a ham sandwich,' the dog seemed to answer.

The proprietor was so impressed by the talking dog that he immediately offered the owner a good sum for it. This was declined, the ventriloquist holding out for a still larger price, which the landlord eventually paid.

As the ventriloquist was leaving the place, the dog turned to him and apparently said: 'You wretch! to sell me for ten pounds! I will never speak another word!'

And he never did.   H. B. S.

PUZZLERS FOR WISE HEADS.

16.—Charade.

My first, it is a thing of worth;
Most men of it have felt a dearth:
It often is the cause of good.
Of warmth and shelter, clothes and food;
It sometimes is the cause of ill,
For folks, to get it, rob and kill.
Its shining, round, and yellow face
Makes it an ornament of grace,
To hang upon a golden chain;
The doctor, with his busy brain,
Receives it often as his fee;
And 'twould be nice for you or me.

My second, whether black or white,
Is looked upon with great delight,
When weeks and months have done their part
In fitting it for shop or mart.
The farmer counts his toil well spent,
The peasant knows he'll pay his rent,
Because my second is so plump
That it can neither run nor jump.

My whole is loved by playful boys
Just grown beyond their childish toys;
And though it wants what dogs and cats,
And mice and rabbits, hares and rats,
And monkeys have, it is a pet
Boys much desire and sometimes get.
                                        C. J. B

17.—Geographical Anagrams.

1. I hem boa. A province of the Austrian Empire; once one of the kingdoms of Europe.
2. Erect. An island in the Mediterranean Sea.
3. Yes, red rib, H. An inland county of England.
4. Eva, Dan. One of the United States of America.

5. Rag than M. A market town in Lincolnshire.
6. Cox, run, same, hut. A well-known village in Sussex.
7. Go, a lad. The largest lake in Europe.
8. Core beam May B. An inlet of the Irish Sea, on the Lancashire coast.
9. O! Marian U. A kingdom in S.E. Europe.
10. Red mat rot. A busy port in Holland.
11. Meal, not gin. A fashionable watering-place.
12. Work thus, A. An old part of London.
                                        C. J. B.

18.—Decapitations.

1. Behead a vehicle, and find a knock at the door.
2. Behead a running stream, and find a noisy bird.
3. Behead a sea-monster, and find an exclamation.
4. Behead an English river, and find something to pay.
5. Behead useful grain, and find caloric.
6. Behead a large nail, and find a greedy fish.
7. Behead part of a machine, and find the hind portion of the foot
8. Behead a dwelling-place, and find a river in Yorkshire.
9. Behead a north countryman, and find a little house.   C. J. B.

[*Answers at page* 106.]

ANSWERS.

14.—1. Marlborough.   5. Winchester.
    2. Rugby.   6. Oxford.
    3. Eton.   7. Cambridge.
    4. Harrow.

15.—1. Endive.   3. Peach.   5. Mint.
    2. Elm.   4. Peas.   6. Beans.

WONDERS OF LITTLE LIVES.

III.—'DEVIL'S COACH-HORSES'; RAFT-SPIDERS; LEAF-CUTTING BEES.

IN my garden a little time ago there was a section of a hollow tree-trunk, destined to form a nesting-place for tit-mice next year. Turning this over, the first thing that met my gaze among the motley crowd of worms, slugs, ants, and so on, which had taken up a residence underneath, was a long and very black beetle, defiantly threatening me with open jaw and uplifted tail. Evidently he expected to frighten me, but failed, for this was by no means my first acquaintance with his kind. Known as the 'Devil's Coach-horse,' he and his friends are to be counted the braggarts among beetles, in this country at any rate. His jet-black colour and the strange attitude which he assumes when disturbed are the signs by which he all men may know him. But this attitude we must hasten to add is by no means his own exclusive mark; it is the attitude and the colour together which make the 'Devil's Coach-horse.' He has many relatives in this country, and they too pose in exactly the same way.

" ' Best bat in the school.' "

Chatterbox (1904)

PHOTO BY CARL COFFMAN

Why, today we don't know where real life is, what it is, or what it's called! Left alone without literature, we immediately become entangled and lost—we don't know what to join, what to keep up with; what to love, what to hate; what to respect, what to despise! We even find it painful to be men—real men of flesh and blood, with our own private bodies; we're ashamed of it, and we long to turn ourselves into something hypothetical called the average man.

—FYODOR DOSTOEVSKI

Photo of a hermit

People seek a central point. That is hard and not even right. I should think a rich, manifold life, brought close to the eyes, would be enough without express tendency; which, after all, is only for the intellect.

—Johann Wolfgang von Goethe

NIGHTMARE . . .

The Power of Beauty;—S.t Cecilia charming the Brute;—or—The seduction of the Welch-Ambassad.
— Pub.d Feb.y 1.st 1792 by H Humphrey N.o 18 Old Bond Street

JAMES GILLRAY (1792)

In the ecstasy of human love, who is unaware that we eat and devour each other, that we long to become part of each other in every way and as the poet said, to carry off even with our teeth the thing we love in order to possess it, feed upon it, become one with it, live on it?

—JACQUES BÉNIGNE BOSSUET

[204]

OR DREAM?

PHOTO BY RON POGUE

lipleafs
pushing
through
Branches singing in the wind
Firnsfur and moss
soft
Skin against skin
speaking to the ears
touch listens
responds
With delicate force
the eyes hear
the taste
the ears
the scent
the feeling
Until All is absorbed

—WILL MAKYNEN

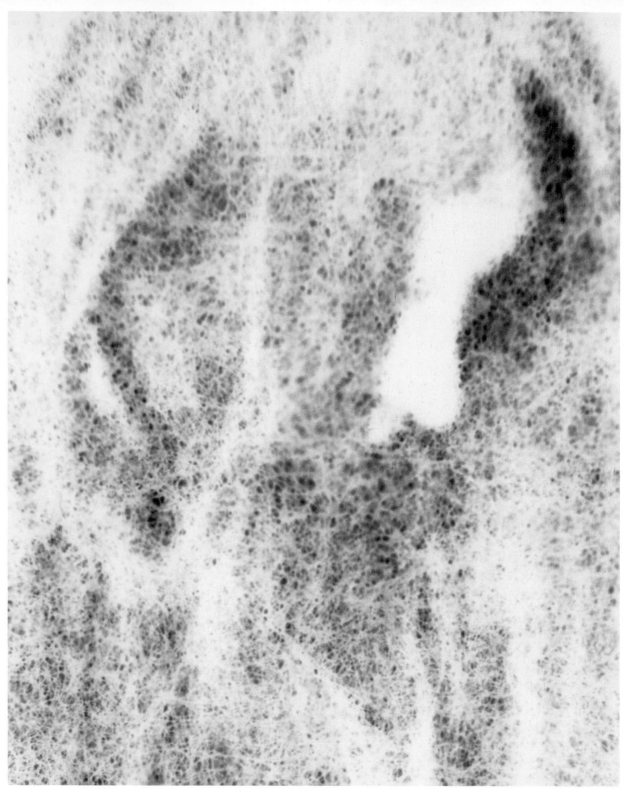

Your hair has reached me like a perfumed hand beckoning me down the ages of the world.

—C. L. WHITE

[206]

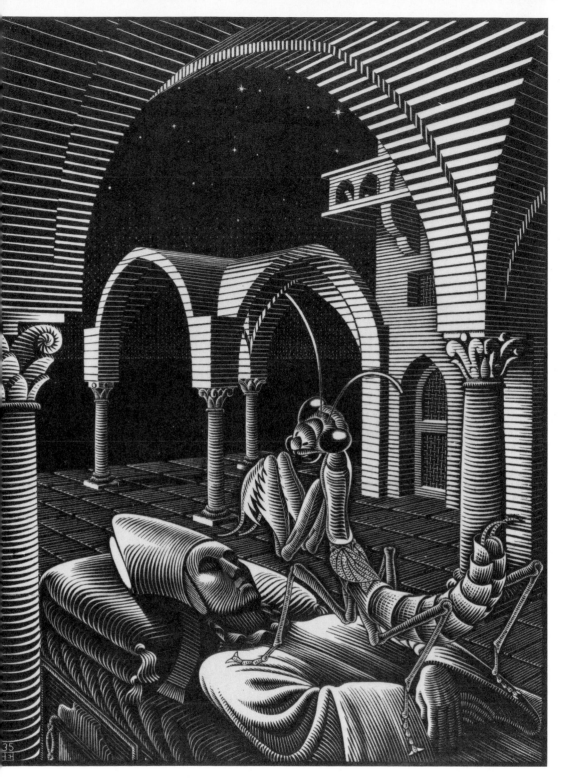

"Dream"   M. C. Escher

Last night I dreamed I was a butterfly
today I am not sure if I am a man
who dreamed he was a butterfly
or a butterfly who dreamed he was a man.

C E N T R A L   P O I N T

•

•

•

there is a terror in silence
that masks it from view
a terror beyond which
only the poet or madman can go

into the silence
that builds silence
into the most eternal poem
into the most lasting insanity

and if you can understand this
you are either a poet or mad

—C. L. WHITE

You say my poems are poetry?
　　They are not.
　　　　Yet if you understand they are not—
　　　　　　Then you see the poetry of them!

—RYÔKAN

"Eye of God"   BY JUDITH WORACEK BARRY

The eye—it cannot choose but see;
We cannot bid the ear be still;
Our bodies feel, where 'er they be,
Against or with our will.

—WILLIAM WORDSWORTH (1770–1850)

"I'd Like to Buy a Ruby Necklace"   BY JUDITH WORACEK BARRY

In a sense, everything is realistic. I
see no line between the imaginary
and the real. I see much reality in
the imaginary.

—FEDERICO FELLINI
Cahiers du Cinema, January 1966

IT IS BECAUSE EVERY ONE
UNDER HEAVEN RECOGNIZES
BEAUTY AS BEAUTY, THAT
THE IDEA OF UGLINESS
EXISTS.

—Tao Tê Ching

Collection, The Museum of Modern Art, New York; gift of J. Kauffmann, Jr.

"Giantess" (1941), *pen and ink, 25 5/8 x 19 7/8"*   GUILLERMO MEZA

"Inferno II"

RON POGUE

. . . Woman is not the useless replica of man, but rather the enchanted place where the living alliance between man and nature is brought about. If she should disappear, men would be alone, strangers lacking passports in an icy world. She is the earth itself raised to life's summit, the earth become sensitive and joyous; and without her, for man the earth is mute and dead.

—MICHEL CARROUGES

I Knew A Woman

I knew a woman lovely in her bones,
When small birds sighed, she would sigh back at them;
Ah, when she moved, she moved more ways than one:
The shapes a bright container can contain!
Of her choice virtues only gods should speak,
Or English poets who grew up on Greek
(I'd have them sing in chorus, cheek to cheek).

How well her wishes went! She stroked my chin,
She taught me turn, and counter-turn, and stand;
She taught me touch, that undulant white skin;
I nibbled meekly from her proffered hand;
She was the sickle; I, poor I, the rake,
Coming behind her for her pretty sake
(But what prodigious mowing we did make).

Love likes a gander, and adores a goose:
Her full lips pursed, the errant note to seize;
She played it quick, she played it light and loose;
My eyes, they dazzled at her flowing knees;
Her several parts could keep a pure repose,
or one hip quiver with a mobile nose
(She moved in circles, and those circles moved).

Let seed be grass, and grass turn into hay:
I'm martyr to a motion not my own;
What's freedom for? to know eternity.
I swear she cast a shadow white as stone
But who would count eternity in days?
These old bones live to learn her wanton ways:
(I measure time by how a body sways).

—Theodore Roethke

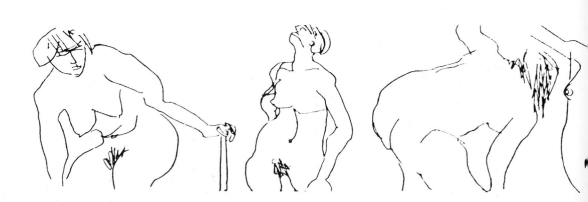

I know the disposition of women: when you will, they won't; when you won't, they set their hearts upon you of their own inclination.

—TERENCE

As the caterpillar chooses the fairest leaves to lay her eggs on, so the priest lays his curse on the fairest joys.

—WILLIAM BLAKE

"Parvati," *bronze sculpture, south Indian, tenth century (detail)*

BY DAN DE VOE (1968)

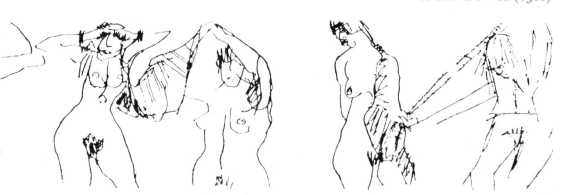

To be a woman is something so strange, so confused, so complicated, that no one predicate comes near expressing it and that the multiple predicates that one would like to use are so contradictory that only a woman could put up with it.

—Sören Kierkegaard

. . . the land is woman and in woman abide the same dark powers as in the earth . . . woman sums up nature as Mother, Wife, and Idea; these forms now mingle and now conflict, and each of them wears a double visage.

—Simone de Beauvoir

PHOTO BY LLOYD DARRAH

FEED
ON
US . . .

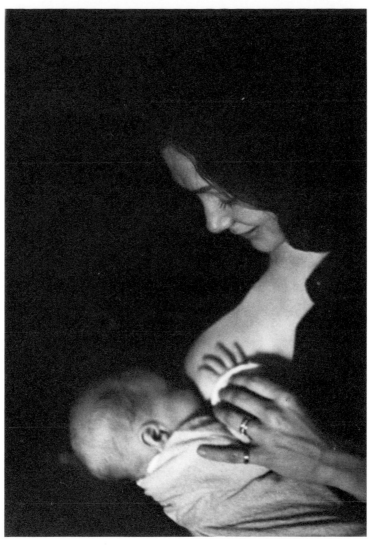

PHOTO BY RON POGUE

Woman does not forget she needs the fecundator, she does not forget that everything that is born of her is planted in her. If she forgets this she is lost. What will be marvelous to contemplate will not be her solitude but this image of woman being visited at night by man and the marvelous things she will give birth to in the morning. God alone, creating, may be a beautiful spectacle. I don't know. Man's objectivity may be an imitation of this God so detached from us and human emotion. But a woman alone creating is not a beautiful spectacle. The woman was born mother, mistress, wife, sister, she was born to give birth to life, and not to insanity. It is man's separateness, his so-called objectivity, which has made him lose contact, and then his reason. Woman was born to be the connecting link between man and his human self. Between abstract ideas and the personal pattern which creates them. Man, to create, must become man.

—ANAÏS NIN, *The Diary of Anaïs Nin*, Vol. 2

THE WOMAN
ARTIST

Woman has this life-role, but the woman artist has to fuse creation and life in her own way, or in her own womb if you prefer. She has to create something different from man. Man created a world cut off from nature. Woman has to create within the mystery, storms, terrors, the infernos of sex, the battle against abstractions and art. She has to sever herself from the myth man creates, from being created by him. She has to struggle with her own cycles, storms, terrors, which man does not understand. Woman wants to destroy aloneness, recover the original paradise. The art of woman must be born in the womb-cells of the mind. She must be the link between the synthetic products of man's mind and the elements.

I do not delude myself as man does, that I create in proud isolation. I say we are bound, interdependent. Woman is not deluded. She must create without these proud delusions of man, without megalomania, without schizophrenia, without madness. She must create that unity which man first destroyed by his proud consciousness.

—ANAÏS NIN, *The Diary of Anaïs Nin,* Vol. 2

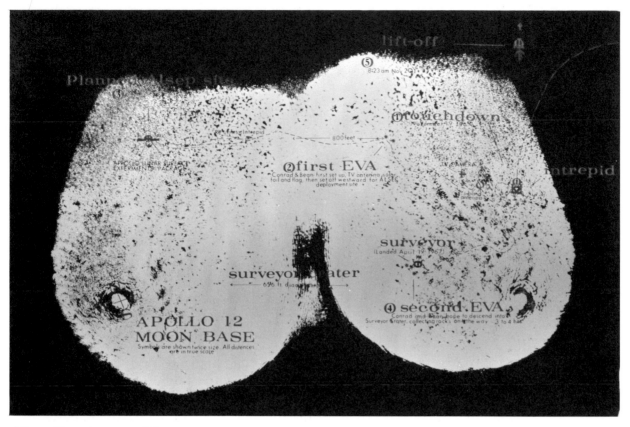

"Landing Approach"   BOBBY STIFFT

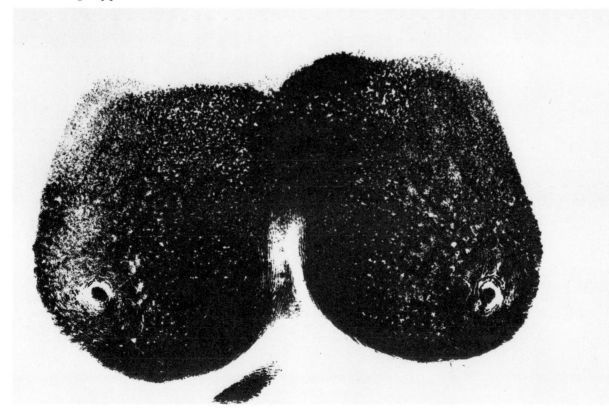

MAN MAKES WOMAN
IN HIS
OWN
IMAGE

She hadde a cok heet Chauntecleer
In al the land of crowing nas his peer.

      ·   ·   ·   ·   ·

His comb was redder than fin coral,
And batailed as it were a castel wal;
His bile was blak, and as the jeet it shoon;
Like asure were his legges and his toon;
His nailes whitter than the lilye flowr,
And lik the burned gold was his colour.

— GEOFFREY CHAUCER, "The Nun's Priest's Tale"

She walks in beauty, like the night
of cloudless climes and starry skies;
And all that's best of dark and bright
Meet in her aspect and her eyes.

— LORD BYRON

From an antique Japanese scroll

"Lady Lilith"

DANTE GABRIEL ROSSETTI

[222]

Man created woman,
and with what?
With the rib of his
god, of his Ideal.

—Friedrich Nietzsche

All walking,
or wandering,
is from mother,
to mother,
in mother,
it gets us
nowhere.

—Norman O. Brown
Love's Body

by C. Owen Smithers

Katherine Ennis (1931)

"Not here!" cried old Walter Gascoigne. "Here, long ago, other mortals built their Temple of Happiness. Seek another site for yours!"

"What!" exclaimed Lilias Fay. "Have any ever planned such a Temple save ourselves?"

"Poor child!" said her gloomy kinsman. "In one shape or other, every mortal has dreamed your dream."

—Nathaniel Hawthorne, "The Lily's Quest"

Miss Katie Hanley (1910)

JOYS IMPREGNATE . . .

PHOTO BY CARL COFFMAN

SORROWS BRING FORTH.

WILLIAM BLAKE, "Proverbs of Hell"

$$t_2' - t_2 = \frac{t_1' - t_1}{\sqrt{1 - \left(\frac{v}{c}\right)^2}}$$

TIME DILATION

PHOTO BY CARL COFFMAN

What is known I strip away,
I launch all men and women forward with me into the Unknown.

The clock indicates the moment—but what does eternity indicate?

We have thus far exhausted trillions of winters and summers,
There are trillions ahead, and trillions ahead of them.

—Walt Whitman, "Song of Myself"

It is only through birth that man can die,

This soil I was everlastingly;
this soil I shall be everlastingly.

—Nikos Kazantzakis

"Verbum"   M. C. Escher

Oh, what a wicked thing it is for flesh
To be the tomb of flesh, for the body's craving
To fatten on the body of another,

For one live creature to continue living
Through one live creature's death.

—Ovid, *Metamorphoses*

Says an old man unable to die,

"With my staff, night and day
I strike on the ground, my
    mother's doorway,
And I say: Ah, mother dear,
            let me in."

—Geoffrey Chaucer

only through death that he can be reborn.

MONTAGE PHOTO BY RON POGUE FROM ORIGINAL PHOTOS BY RON POGUE AND CARL COFFMAN

Head of Aphrodite, style of Praxiteles

THE WORLD IS

Let's love, this life of ours
Can make no truce with time that all devours.
Let's love: the sun doth set, and rise againe
But when as our short light
Comes once to set, it makes eternall night.

—Samuel Daniel (1562–1619)

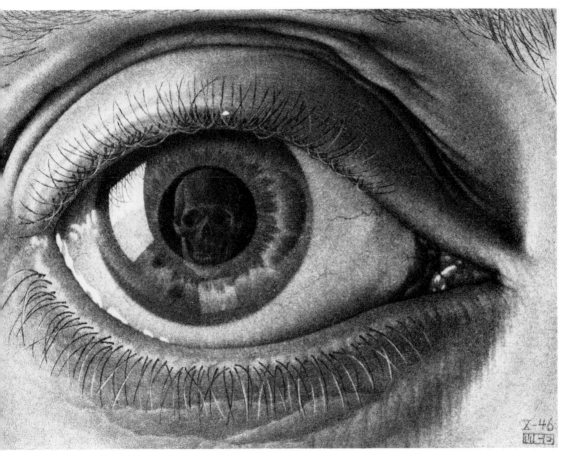

by M. C. Escher

TREMBLING

We must act *as if* the world were on the verge of extinction. —REINHOLD NIEBUHR

Then he waited, marshaling his thoughts and brooding over his still untested powers. For though he was master of the world, he was not quite sure what to do next.

But he would think of something.

—ARTHUR C. CLARKE, *2001: A Space Odyssey*

Soft moccasinned strangers
in black velvet night
came
and gave me two nestlings —
nighthawks, they were.
I grew patient
    watching them sleep.
I grew wise
    watching them eat,
and I grew old
    setting them free.

                    —Dona Ware
                    age 17
                    Billings,
                    Montana

PHOTOS BY CARL COFFMAN